ELLIS ISLAND

Gateway of Hope

by
John Burdick

SMITHMARK

The author and editors gratefully acknowledge the help of Jeffrey S. Dosick and Barry Moreno of the Ellis Island Research Library, and Geraldine Santoro, Curator of Collections, Ellis Island Immigration Museum, as well as Peg Zitko of The Statue of Liberty–Ellis Island Foundation.

This edition published in 1997 by SMITHMARK Publishers, a division of U.S. Media Holdings, Inc., 16 East 32nd Street, New York, NY 10016.

SMITHMARK books are available for bulk purchase for sales promotion and premium use. For details write or call the manager of special sales, SMITHMARK Publishers, 16 East 32nd Street, New York, NY 10016; (212) 532-6600.

This book was designed and produced by Todtri Productions Limited P.O. Box 572, New York, NY 10116-0572 FAX: (212) 279-1241

Printed and bound in Singapore

Library of Congress Catalog Card Number 96-71467
ISBN 0-7651-9426-0

Author: John Burdick

Publisher: Robert M. Tod
Editorial Director: Elizabeth Loonan
Senior Editor: Cynthia Sternau
Project Editor: Ann Kirby
Photo Editor: Edward Douglas
Picture Researchers: Heather Weigel, Laura Wyss
Production Coordinator: Annie Kaufmann
Designer: Creative Studio Editions

Picture Credits

Contents

Introduction

odern America begins at Ellis Island, the Plymouth Rock of the twentieth century. Between 1892 and 1954, over twelve million people passed through the Ellis Island federal immigrant receiving station. In the peak years of 1900–1914, they sometimes arrived at a rate of seven thousand per day. Hundreds of thousands more were turned away. Today, roughly half of the population of the United States can trace its ancestry through the immigrants processed on this mostly man-made island, inspected in the Great Hall, ferried across New York Harbor on the S.S. *Ellis Island*, and, from New York City, transported to cities and towns across the country.

One of the great human dramas of the nineteenth and twentieth centuries, the mass migration to America transpired on the most unlikely of stages. A low-lying, minuscule sandbar between Manhattan and New Jersey, Samuel Ellis' island was known to disappear from view at high tide. If Treasury Secretary William Windom had not reluctantly chosen it as the site for an immigration center, Ellis Island would have gone down in history as little more than a fisherman's paradise and a minor, supporting player in two nineteenth-century wars.

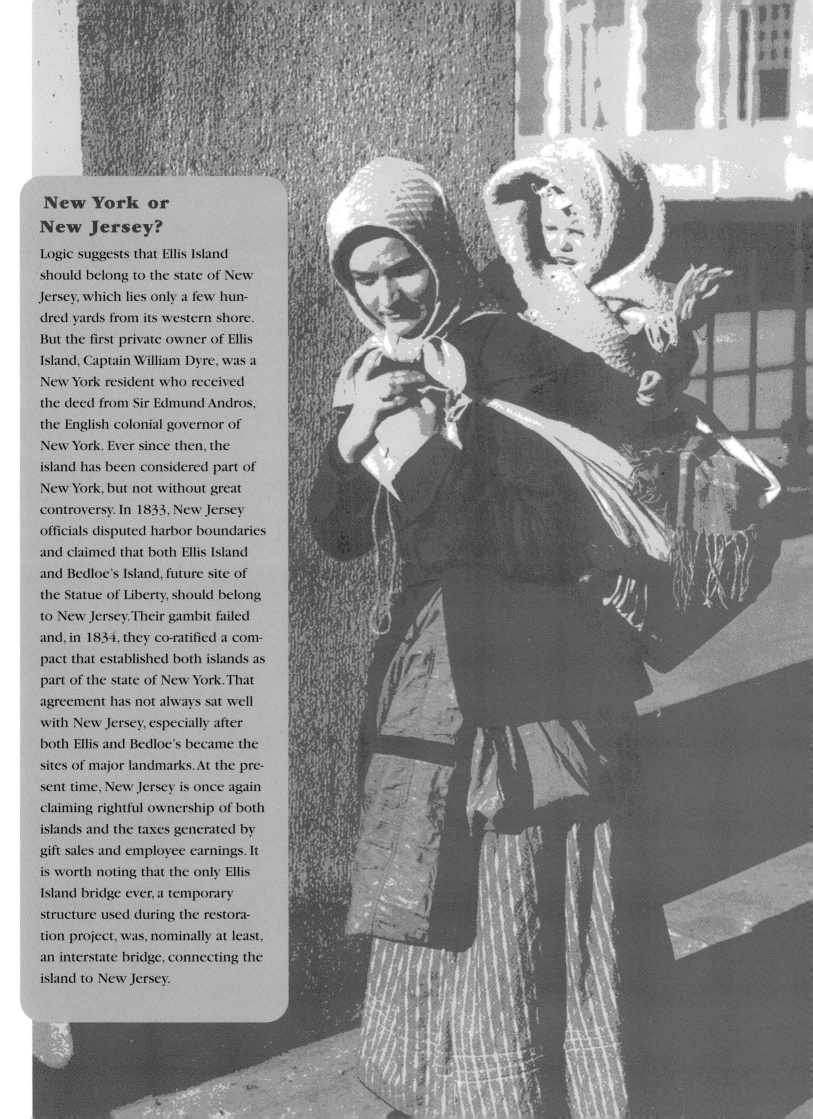

New York or New Jersey?

Logic suggests that Ellis Island should belong to the state of New Jersey, which lies only a few hundred yards from its western shore. But the first private owner of Ellis Island, Captain William Dyre, was a New York resident who received the deed from Sir Edmund Andros, the English colonial governor of New York. Ever since then, the island has been considered part of New York, but not without great controversy. In 1833, New Jersey officials disputed harbor boundaries and claimed that both Ellis Island and Bedloe's Island, future site of the Statue of Liberty, should belong to New Jersey. Their gambit failed and, in 1834, they co-ratified a compact that established both islands as part of the state of New York. That agreement has not always sat well with New Jersey, especially after both Ellis and Bedloe's became the sites of major landmarks. At the present time, New Jersey is once again claiming rightful ownership of both islands and the taxes generated by gift sales and employee earnings. It is worth noting that the only Ellis Island bridge ever, a temporary structure used during the restoration project, was, nominally at least, an interstate bridge, connecting the island to New Jersey.

ELLIS ISLAND

Fate had bigger plans, however, and today, American history and Ellis Island are inextricably linked. Trends and shifts in immigration law and public opinion were played out in the daily business of immigrant processing. The larger debates and conflicting ideals that defined America reverberated in the Great Hall registry room. Officials at Ellis Island made decisions in which all Americans felt they should have some say: whom to admit, whom to reject, and why. The island came to symbolize, to some, the dangerous leniency of immigration policy, to others the noblest and most ambitious American principles. When Ellis Island closed in 1954, after years of dwindling activity, an American era closed with it.

History, Ellis Island reminds us, does not live only in dates and statistics but in the unique stories and voices of individuals as well. In these, Ellis Island is incomparably rich. Often called "the island of hope and the island of tears," Ellis Island is perhaps the most symbolically complex of all American landmarks. It may never have existed if the tragedies of famine, war, persecution, and oppression had not driven millions from their homelands. Yet it is quite certain that America as we know it would not exist if not for the energy, talent, and intelligence that the millions brought with them. Today's Ellis Island, a beautifully restored museum and educational center, honors the immigrants, the ordeals they endured, and the great contributions they made.

The themes of light and dark, hope and fear, compassion and suspicion, and joy and sorrow intermingle in the history of United States immigration. In vivid and human detail, Ellis Island tells the story of America's ideals and realities. If the neighboring Statue of Liberty represents the American promise in its purest and simplest form, Ellis Island reminds us of the immense difficulty of putting that promise into action, the compromises, the contradictions, the hard-earned triumphs. The Statue of Liberty tells the story we like to hear; Ellis Island tells the story we need to hear.

Ellis Island
Before the Flood

CHAPTER ONE

Turn-of-the-century New York was the gateway to America for millions of immigrants processed at Castle Garden, and later on, at Ellis Island. Though many immigrants traveled on to other parts of the country, a great many settled in New York City soon after disembarking, creating a rich ethnic mosaic that still thrives in the city.

Although Ellis Island would become the site and symbol of one of the most remarkable periods of immigration in history, the island itself as it appeared to the early European settlers was entirely unremarkable. Nothing about it suggested the tremendous significance it would assume in the nineteenth and twentieth centuries. A mere three sandy acres in New York Harbor, Ellis Island was considered by the Indians, the Dutch, and the English to be uninhabitable. The shallow surrounding waters made access difficult for ships. Frequently bought and sold, used and abandoned, named and renamed, the island's only consistent tenants for centuries were the seagulls that thrived on its oyster-rich shoals. Even as late as the nineteenth century, when federal officials sought a new site for an immigration center to replace the

RIGHT: *On a bleak and rainy day in October of 1886, the Statue of Liberty was unveiled before a crowd estimated at over one million. In the decades that followed, the statue would become the first glimpse of America for the millions of immigrants processed at the receiving station on nearby Ellis Island.*

LEFT: *Land, Ho! Passengers aboard an emigrant ship stop what they are doing to catch their first glimpse of America.*

congested and overwhelmed Castle Garden, Ellis Island was chosen only because the preferred location, nearby Bedloe's Island, was already busy with the Statue of Liberty. Still, simply by virtue of being in New York, where a purpose was found for every place no matter how obscure, Ellis Island has a history of various uses and curious anecdotes prior to the construction of the first immigrant receiving station in the 1890s.

An Island of Many Names

The earliest recorded names of Ellis Island reflect the common opinion that it was a place unfit for humans and best left to the animals, a judgment that would, ironically, reappear centuries later when some social commentators decried the inhumane treatment of immigrants at the receiving station. Before the arrival of the Dutch and the English, the Mohegan Indians called it Kioshk, or Gull Island. In the early 1600s, the first Dutch settlers, following the lead of the explorer Henry Hudson, began arriving and occupying territories along the Hudson River and on Long Island. The Dutch West India Company purchased Gull Island from the Mohegans and, recognizing its chief commercial value, renamed it Little Oyster Island. Although it was used primarily for the harvesting of oysters and the drying of fishing nets, some wealthy Dutchmen found it an attractive spot for picnics and parties.

The Dutch settlers, however, had little occasion for leisure. Their attempt at colonization was short-lived and fraught with danger and difficulty. By the 1660s, the Dutch had all but abandoned the area. The English swept into the harbor and, encountering little resistance, claimed the colony. New Amsterdam became New York. Still thought to be little more than a good place for oysters, Ellis Island changed hands and names frequently through the next one hundred years. The first recorded private owner, Captain William Dyre, was a resident and onetime mayor of New York City. In 1686, Dyre's Island was sold to Thomas and Patience Lloyd. Lloyd's Island later became Bucking Island. In 1757, Bucking Island was briefly considered as the site of a prospective city pest house. Finally, on November 18, 1774, Samuel Ellis of 1 Greenwich Street, Manhattan, purchased the island and lent it his name.

ABOVE: *The Statue of Liberty was a gift of the people of France, and symbolized the American promise of freedom and opportunity for all. For immigrants entering New York Harbor, like those pictured in this 1886 engraving, the statue was the first sign that they had finally arrived.*

Ellis, a farmer and merchant originally from New Jersey, used the island as a tavern for fishermen. The business, apparently, was not sufficiently interesting or lucrative for Ellis. In 1785, he advertised the sale of his island in *Loudon's New York Packet*. There were no buyers. In 1794, Samuel Ellis died. He willed the island to his daughter Catherine's child, provided that the child was a boy and bore the name of Samuel Ellis. Catherine's son Samuel died in infancy. Ownership reverted to Catherine, and the island of many names and few uses stayed in the Ellis family until 1808.

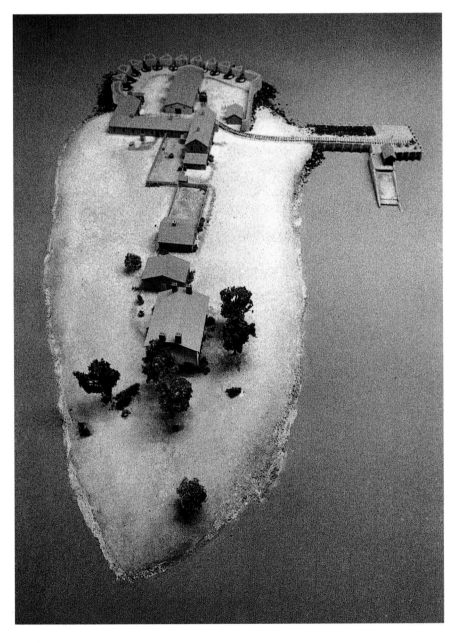

LEFT: *This model depicts Ellis Island during its years as Fort Gibson in the mid-nineteenth century. Over the years, the small island would be enlarged from three to twenty-seven acres to accommodate the immigrant receiving station.*

RIGHT: *Women and children frequently traveled to America together, months or even years after the men of the family had established themselves in the New World.*

A New Landlord: The U.S. Government Buys Ellis Island

History would not immortalize Ellis Island for years to come, but in the early nineteenth century, it briefly became a place of interest to more than just fishermen. Responding to political instability in Europe and the danger it posed to the bustling New York Harbor trade, New York State allocated a large sum of money to fortify the harbor islands. Bedloe's Island, Governor's Island, and Ellis Island were all chosen for fortifications, but because of confusion surrounding the ownership of Ellis Island, construction there was postponed.

In 1808, with tensions rising between the United States and England, the U.S. Government purchased Ellis Island for the sum $10,183.10, an acquisition that paved the way for all future public uses of the island. Built between 1808 and 1811, the newly christened Fort Gibson became the site of a thirteen-gun battery and a magazine (a warehouse in which explosive powders are stored). Fortified for combat, Fort Gibson's actual involvement in the War of 1812 was minimal. Apparently, the intimidating specter of the harbor forts was enough to deter invaders. Fort Gibson was used to house some American soldiers and, in a role it would reprise in World War I and World War II, to detain prisoners of war.

After the war, Fort Gibson was maintained but rarely used, and the island once again lay dormant. Some recruits were trained there. Following a practice established in the eighteenth century, the island was occasionally the site of pirate hangings. Larger weapons had allowed harbor fortifications to move out of the lower harbor area and further away from land. No longer instrumental in harbor security, Fort Gibson was deacti-

LEFT: *Emigrants departing for America bid farewell to family and friends. Often, entire families could not afford to cross at once, so fathers or oldest children would travel alone, promising their loved ones a reunion in America.*

RIGHT: *Transporting immigrants was an enormously profitable business. Steamship companies made a fortune, though the accommodations offered were not always as advertised.*

The Notorious Anderson

Perhaps the least savory part of Ellis Island's pre-immigration history has nothing to do with spoiled oysters but with the occasional practice of hanging pirates. In 1765, the notorious pirate Anderson was hanged there, and for a while after, Ellis became known as either Anderson's Island or Gibbets Island, after an archaic term for gallows. Ellis Island may have been a popular site for pirate hangings because of its highly visible location in New York Harbor. Hanged pirates were prominently displayed on the gibbets to dissuade any would-be pirates entering the harbor, in much the same way that the mere sight of the Fort Gibson battery served to dissuade English invaders during the War of 1812. Even after Ellis Island was taken over by the federal government in 1808, pirate hangings continued—two in 1831 and one, murderer Cornelius Wilhelms, in 1839. Old habits die hard.

vated in 1835 and dismantled in 1861. In its place, the U.S. Navy constructed a magazine that would soon be put to use in the Civil War as a dispatching center for shells and powder. This seems to typify Ellis Island's place in the first three centuries of American history: occasionally involved but always on the outskirts, a historical footnote were it not for the remarkable transformation it would undergo in the 1890s.

Meanwhile, at Castle Garden . . .

New York City had long been the most alluring and active port of entry into what was, for Europeans, the "new world." While the more provincial colonies and states were wary of immigrants, especially those newcomers who spoke different languages and practiced strange customs, New York thrived on and welcomed diversity. In the mid-to-late nineteenth century, roughly seventy percent of immigrants from Europe passed through

RIGHT: *Russian emigrants land at New York's Barge Office in 1892. The bearded older man at the front of the line might have had a difficult time convincing authorities that he was physically capable of supporting himself once in America.*

New York. Most were received and processed at Castle Garden in lower Manhattan, just a short distance from the quiet Ellis Island naval magazine. Itself an attempt to centralize the hectic business of immigration in New York, as Ellis Island would later be, Castle Garden opened in 1855 and, in its first year, admitted over 50,000 immigrants.

The Civil War slowed the tide of immigration considerably, and Castle Garden appeared to be an adequate facility. Immediately following the war, however, immigration skyrocketed, surpassing in four years the total of the previous decade. Because of industrialization and westward expansion, job opportunities grew at an unprecedented rate. Some companies involved in the development of the western frontier actually recruited immigrant labor overseas, a practice that would soon end due to Alien Contract Labor Law of 1885 and growing national alarm over the immigration issue.

Under an unexpected siege, problems with Castle Garden soon became apparent. By the 1880s, the facility was simply not large enough to handle the rush of immigrants. It was overtaxed and, importantly, under-supervised. Immigrants, especially those who did not speak English and those who were not met by relatives, were easy prey. The Castle Garden pier teemed with all kinds of scam artists, runners hired by local boarding houses, and fraudulent transportation agents. The bewildered new arrivals were often deceived, misled, and overcharged. Even more disturbing were reports of bribery and corruption among the Castle Garden employees.

ABOVE: In the Land of Promise—Castle Garden *(Charles Frederic Ulrich, 1884) depicts a peasant woman feeding her child while awaiting inspection at Castle Garden. In the nineteenth century, the name of Castle Garden was so famous in Europe that immigrants who had actually passed through Ellis Island would claim with certainty in later years that they had been processed at Castle Garden.*

Rejection at Castle Garden

From the *East Boston Argus Advocate,* May 28, 1887:

The floor of [Castle Garden] is railed off into numerous pens, and the immigrants pass from one to another, and eventually outside the building, if they pass examination, by going through alleyways where officers station themselves to ask the necessary questions. When the reporter arrived one-half the floor was getting its forenoon thrashing with mops and brooms, and the immigrants were confined in the pens on the other side. The whole floor is washed thoroughly twice every day, and, considering the heterogeneous masses of people who are always there, the place is clean and healthy . . .

In the garden at the time of the reporter's visit was a family of Russian Jews who had arrived the night before. They had been detained until the Commissioner should render a formal decision upon them. Not one of them could be called able-bodied. They were infirm, knew no trade, had been at the best but peddlers in Russia, which meant beggars, were ragged, dirty, wretched to the last degree, had not as much as a cent of money, and were without relatives or friends here. The representative of the Hebrew Immigrants' Aid Society had talked with them, but even he, with all the race devotion which characterizes the Jews, could not bring himself to say that he would see that they became self-supporting members of the community. A decision had been quickly reached, and presently it was communicated officially to the group. They could not understand a word of English, but they had been told that there was great doubt of their being allowed to land. . . . They watched the reading with the most painful interest, mouths open, hands upraised, and when it had been concluded and the interpreter had told them in one word its meaning, the fell into the most extravagant lamentation. The leader of the party, an old man whose toes protruded from his boots, fell upon the floor and tried to embrace the official's knees while supplicating him in unintelligible jargon. . . . It was altogether a most pitiable spectacle.

It was also in the late nineteenth century that national attitudes toward immigration began to change, a trend that would continue even through the peak years of Ellis Island immigration. Government officials called for stricter immigration regulations and more thorough and tough-minded examinations. For reasons familiar to Americans of today, public sentiment began to turn from welcoming to wary: foreigners willing to work at low wages might fill too many of the jobs available to established citizens; the absence of careful scrutiny, some thought, threatened national welfare by allowing in the infirm and the "mentally defective," those least able to take care of themselves and most likely to become public charges.

ABOVE: *Immigrants in Ellis Island, circa 1895. Like many of the better-informed immigrants, the woman on the left brought food from home for both the ocean passage and the long waits at the receiving station.*

These two concerns—one for the well-being of the immigrants, the other for the well-being of the country in the face of a perceived threat—led to increased federal involvement in immigration policy and procedure, formerly the domain of individual states. A congressional investigation of Castle Garden in 1888 determined that both the facility and its procedures were unsatisfactory. The government began plans for the first federally-operated immigration center. In 1889, the federal government assumed sole control of immigration in New York, two years before it would extend its authority over immigration in all states. In 1890, William D. Owen, a congressman from Indiana, became the first Superintendent of Immigration, a new post to be overseen by the Secretary of the Treasury. On April 11, 1890, acting on the recommendation of Treasury Secretary William Windom, President Benjamin Harrison approved Ellis Island as the site of the new immigrant receiving station.

RIGHT: *These German immigrants, unfamiliar with English and thus unable to follow signs, relied on strangers to find their way to the train station. Not all strangers were friendly, and immigrants were easy marks for scam artists and frauds.*

1892 and 1900: Two Receiving Stations

For Secretary Windom and his colleagues, the decision had not been an easy one. Situated in shallow water as it was, Ellis Island would be difficult if not impossible to approach in a large ship. The low-lying land, a porous clay, did not bode well for the kind of structures required. In fact, Ellis Island was commended solely by its availability. When Windom proposed Bedloe's Island, home of the Statue of Liberty, he was met with public outrage and the scorn of Frederic Auguste Bartholdi, the French designer of the statue. Windom's other preferred location, the much larger Governor's Island, had long been the site of an important army installation.

In Ellis Island, Windom found a site that, at the very least, would not provoke public resistance. Quite the opposite, in fact. In the years following the Civil War, the navy magazine on Ellis Island had been the subject of recurrent public controversies. In 1868 an alarming article in *Harper's Weekly* informed local residents that the volatile munitions dump was dangerously close to businesses and residences in New Jersey, a disaster waiting to happen. Similar *New York Sun* and *New York World* reports followed in the 1870s. Soon thereafter, a New Jersey senator called for the removal of the Ellis Island magazine. Thus, despite Ellis Island's physical inadequacies, local reaction to the proposed immigration station there ranged from indifference to relief.

ABOVE: *The Castle Garden immigrant receiving station, shown at the left in Samuel Waugh's* **The Bay and Harbor of New York** *(1855) was in operation from 1855 through the opening of Ellis Island in 1892, processing a large influx of mostly Irish, German, and English immigrants. (Courtesy of the Museum of the City of New York.)*

RIGHT: *A White Star Line poster from the turn of the century announces sailings between Naples and New York and Boston. Ship companies often advertised comfortable quarters and plentiful food, false promises for the majority of immigrants who traveled in the miserable steerage compartments.*

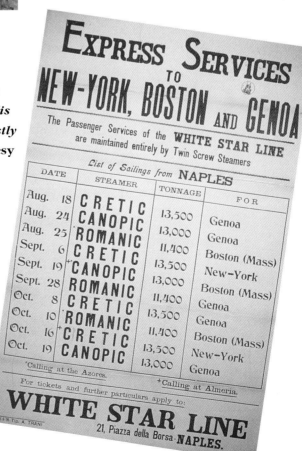

Blown into Atoms

From *Harper's Weekly,* March 14, 1868:

The New York Sun lately called attention to the startling fact that New York, Brooklyn, Jersey City, and the numerous villages on Staten Island, are now, and have been for a long time, in imminent peril of being at once destroyed by the explosions of the magazines on Ellis' Island, which lies in New York Harbor, about half-way between the Battery and the New Jersey shore. We have had a sketch made of the island, and after some inquiries into the facts of the case, find that the fears of the Sun are well-founded; the million and a half people residing in the vicinity of the City Hall of New York are daily and hourly in imminent danger of being blown into atoms!

. . . It has been clearly demonstrated by a simple arithmetical calculation, based on actual experiments, that the gas generated by a sudden combustion of 1500 hundred tons of powder would exert, at a distance of eight miles, a pressure of 200 pounds to the square yard. Within eight miles of Ellis Island lies all of Jersey City, all of Brooklyn, and all of the populous part of New York below Central Park. Every building in either of these cities has a frontage of at least 150 square yards, and would, therefore, in case of an explosion, receive a sudden shock of 30,000 pounds, before which the stoutest wall would instantly give way.

A great deal of precaution is taken to prevent any accidents on the Island . . . the magazines are plentifully supplied with lightening-rods; great care is taken in handling the powder; the workmen wear canvas shoes and are not allowed to carry pocket-knives or other steel or iron implements. . . . But still the greatest precautions are sometimes in vain. There is not the slightest necessity for accumulating this amount of powder in such close proximity to the most populous city in the country. . . . It is a subject which we should imagine might be of interest enough to the municipality of New York to prompt an emphatic protest.

ABOVE: *The original Ellis Island main building was constructed of Georgia Pine in 1892 and leveled by fire in 1897. During the reconstruction of the Ellis Island station, immigrants were received at the Manhattan Barge Office, the predecessor to Castle Garden.*

June 4th — 1897.

Construction took place between 1890 and 1892. After the removal of the munitions dump, the island was expanded from three to fourteen acres, the first of many such additions. Popular (and probably trustworthy) rumor had it that the landfill used to extend the island came from New York City subway tunnels in progress. Officials determined that five of the existing buildings on the island were worth keeping. Seven new buildings were designed and constructed, including the first hospital, a powerhouse, and the massive main building, designed by the New York firm of Sheridan & Byrne. Described by the *New York Times* as a building "of no particular style of architecture," the main building was constructed almost entirely of Georgia pine, an expensive, strong, and, of course, flammable wood. The station opened on January 1, 1892, the day on which three steamships delivered a total of seven hundred passengers. Recurrent doubts about the structural soundness and permanence of the building proved to be warranted when, in 1897, a fire leveled the main building, making way for a more durable and lasting structure.

The Miraculous Growing Island

1890–1892
As part of the construction of the first immigration station, Ellis Island is expanded form three to fourteen acres.

1898–1899
After a fire destroys the first immigration center, Ellis Island is expanded to seventeen acres in the rebuilding process. Island 2 is created.

1901
Kitchen, bathhouse, and laundry buildings built on Island 1.

1902
A hospital is erected on Island 2.

1905–1906
More landfill from New York City subway excavations is used to create the five-acre Island 3.

1909
Contagious Disease Ward built on Island 3.

1913–1915
Bakery, greenhouse, and carpenter's shop are built on Island 1.

1934
Ellis Island is increased to its present size of 27.5 acres.

In the years after the fire, New York immigration operations returned to Manhattan's Barge Office, the predecessor of Castle Garden. Overcrowding and inadequate facilities at the Barge Office left no doubt that the Ellis Island facility should be restored. It would take only three years for a larger, fireproof main building to take shape. Designed by the firm of Boring & Tilton, the new French Renaissance structure was begun in December of 1897. Featuring four towers topped with copper domes and spires and an attractive brick and limestone facade, the main building was considered by many to be an architectural masterwork in an old world style.

The interior facilities were also improved, fortified to handle the ever-increasing numbers of immigrants at the turn of the century. Once again, the island was enlarged, this time from fourteen to seventeen acres, to make room for several new buildings including a large kitchen, a bathhouse, and a laundry building. On opening day, December 17, 1900, the *Kaiser Wilhelm II* landed at the new Ellis Island. A total of 2,251 immigrants were processed that day, a seemingly huge number at the time but only a meek foreshadowing of the deluge that would follow.

Isle of Tears

Over twelve million immigrants passed through Ellis Island between 1892 and 1954, sometimes arriving at a rate of seven thousand per day. With them came twelve million individual stories, twelve million hopes and dreams, all woven into the tapestry of modern American history.

Her name was Annie Moore, a fifteen-year-old girl from County Cork in Ireland and the first immigrant to pass through the Ellis Island receiving station. Moore was greeted with a modest ceremony, a speech by the New York Commissioner of Immigration, Colonel John B. Weber, and the presentation of a $10 gold piece. For the 699 other arrivals on January 1, 1892, for the 444,000 of that year, and for the millions upon millions in the decades to come, there would be no such welcome, no financial head start. For most immigrants Ellis Island represented the fearsome and prolonged moment of truth, a purgatory in which their dreams of freedom and opportunity would be realized or be dashed. These were courageous and strong people, strong enough to leave their ancestral homes at

considerable cost and risk, strong enough to endure the ocean voyage in the filthy and infamous steerage compartment. But upon arrival at Ellis Island, their fate was out of their hands. With the criteria for acceptance and rejection in a state of constant flux, they could not prepare for the inspection to follow. They could not know that at the top of the stairs to the Great Hall, doctors observed the exhausted passengers as they ascended, looking for lameness, shortness of breath, anything that might indicate physical unfitness. They could not will themselves in, no matter how strong their wills.

To the immigrants, Ellis Island was a gateway, simultaneously inviting and forbidding, located not between New York and New Jersey but precisely halfway between the old world and the new. Though Manhattan

ABOVE: *The* **S.S. Ellis Island,** *a modern-day version of the original Ellis Island ferry, approaches the ferry landing. Today, tourists aboard the ferry follow the same route as the immigrants did.*

and the Statue of Liberty were clearly visible from the shores of Ellis Island, the Europe they left, the homes that for many no longer existed and the governments and empires that would not take kindly to their emigration, were just as close, just as imminent. After the exhausting ordeals, the separation from loved ones, the examinations, and, always, the waiting, an overwhelming majority made it through. Individually, these are stories of heroism, courage and sacrifice; collectively, in their millions, they form the story of America, of a promise—incomplete, messy, and not always fair—made good.

BELOW: *Steamship companies often used popular American symbolism in their advertisements, luring immigrants with the promise of freedom and opportunity.*

The Land of Milk and Honey

From the first minute that I got here I realized that I am a free man . . . I have a fighting chance to make a living. That means everything. I didn't realize it as much as I do now, but at the time it was a big thrill.

—*Sam Birnbaum, a Polish immigrant in 1907, interviewed in 1985.*

[The United States was] . . . the land of milk and honey, and . . . you can pick up money on the street, just waiting for you. It's a garden, still growing.

—*Philip Bornstein, Lithuanian immigrant, 1921.*

I wish you to come to America, dear brother, because up to the present I am doing very well here, and I have no intention of going to our country, because in our country I experienced only misery and poverty, and now I live better than a lord in our country.

—*Letter from Adam Raczkowski to his cousin-in-law Teofil Wolski in Poland, 1906.*

The Immigrants

Some fled poverty, oppression and starvation. Some left due to restlessness, the urge west, and the desire to escape the rigidity of the European social class structure. Some came to re-invent themselves on the new continent, others to restore the traditions and practices that had been denied and punished at home. Some families came all at once, but most came in waves: fathers first, followed by children old enough to work, followed, finally, by wives and small children. In some cases, teenagers traveling alone led the way, staking a claim in America while their parents continued to work and save to bring the rest of the family across. The reasons for coming and the routes followed were

ABOVE: *Women traveling with children faced additional difficulties. They had to convince officials that they would not become charity cases, in many instances enduring detention at Ellis Island while they waited for family members or sponsors to meet them.*

as many and various as the people who came, but most had in common the destination, and the ordeal, of Ellis Island.

Concurrent with the opening of Ellis Island was a significant change in the character and origins of the immigrants. The early and mid-nineteenth century immigrants had been predominantly western and northern Europeans: the English, Irish, Germans, and Scandinavians. Their passage from Europe was harrowing, but acceptance into America, at Castle Garden

Streets of Gold

That's all you heard. Gold on the streets of America. . . . There's no North America and no South America, not United States, just America. It was all good things. You could be anything you want here and make a lot of money, even if it was a dollar a day.

—Louise Nagy, Polish immigrant in 1913

I came to America because I heard the streets were paved with gold. When I got here, I found out three things: first, the streets weren't paved with gold; second, they weren't paved at all; and third, I was expected to pave them.

—Old Italian story

or at ports in other cities, was relatively assured. Those were the days of seemingly limitless resources and largely unregulated immigration. Furthermore, for many of these passengers there was some degree of cultural familiarity and opportunity. There was also the plausible prospect of return to family, friends, land, and businesses in the old world.

The new immigrants, those who would flock to Ellis Island in the early twentieth century, came mostly from central, eastern, and southern Europe. They were Poles, Czechs, Ukrainians, Italians, Greeks, and many others fleeing the oppression of autocratic empires, rural poverty, urban abjection, and official attempts to squash diversity of religion, language, and culture. Many fled nothing less than death. Jews escaped the

ABOVE: *The most recognized external features of the Ellis Island main building are its four copper spires and domes placed atop brick and limestone towers. The original spires were decayed beyond repair by the time restoration efforts began, and had to be replaced.*

LEFT: *An Italian family aboard the S.S. Ellis Island. Immigrants often faced long waits to board ferries and even longer waits once on them.*

RIGHT: *This German poster from the early 1900s warns women of the dangers of traveling alone in a foreign country. Such fears were made into policy at Ellis Island. Unescorted women were not allowed to leave the island, for fear they would be lured into prostitution. Such "marriageable" women would often be met by suitors at Ellis Island.*

massacres known as pogroms. Armenians, the lucky ones, escaped genocide by the Turks. And all who escaped, perhaps through some kind of collective prescience, escaped the impending upheaval of World War I. For most of these immigrants, there would be nothing to which they could return.

Whether by word from those who had already emigrated or by rumors of gold-paved streets and limitless wealth, they were drawn to America. In Europe the name and figure of Abraham Lincoln represented freedom, opportunity, and equality. America also represented adventure, prospects of growth and advancement that simply were not possible within the old and established

classifications of European society. Most immigrants, however, were not naive. Stories of triumph and of failure made their way back to Europe. They understood well the dangers of immigration and the uncertainties that awaited them in America. They were, at heart, gamblers. Immigration was a once-in-a-lifetime proposition, expensive, dangerous, and, usually, unrepeatable. Acceptance meant a chance at a new life in a prospering and open country; rejection meant a grim and destitute return to worsening social and economic conditions in Europe.

ABOVE: *At the end of their long sea journey, immigrants were faced with another journey through the maze of processing. Passing through long and slow moving lines under the canopy, the immigrants would make their way to the front entrance and into the large first floor baggage room.*

RIGHT: *The North German Lloyd liner* **Kronprinzessin Cecilie** *was one of the many great ships that brought immigrants to the New World.*

The Journey

It was a journey of many stages, each with its own risks and uncertainties. The first task was among the most challenging: to somehow amass the money necessary to travel and to settle in America. Most immigrants were poor. Bare subsistence at home had been almost impossibly expensive; emigrating was exorbitant. The overland journey to the port cities often required the bribery of border guards in addition to train fare, if train travel was even possible. Once in the port cities, those with tickets in advance usually boarded quickly. Those without, especially in later years when the United States imposed annual national quotas on immigration, might be sent home poorer than when they left because they were a month, a week, a day too late.

D. „Kronprinzessin Cecilie"

Still, they flocked to the major European ports: Piraeus in Greece, Naples in Italy, Hamburg in Germany, Marseilles in France. After solitary and stealthy travel, social interaction in the port cities was a joy and a relief. Certainly, there were continued difficulties. There were tickets to acquire, papers to obtain, and, in the years after the United States shifted much of the burden of inspection onto the steamship companies, examinations and inspections to endure. But many immigrants recall the few days or weeks spent waiting for a ship as a welcomed respite spent with fellow travelers, a brief calm between tumultuous journeys.

ABOVE: *This Yiddish circular, distributed in Russia by the Jewish Colonization Association, described job opportunities and connections available in Massachusetts.*

RIGHT: *Spontaneous artworks such as this bird scratched in a wall were a natural product of the long and anxiety-ridden delays endured by the immigrants.*

ABOVE: *Most immigrants traveled in the cheap steerage compartment of the trans-Atlantic ships. Crowded quarters, poor ventilation, and stormy weather made steerage an uncomfortable and sometimes dangerous experience.*

And the ocean passage certainly was tumultuous. For the European steamship companies, mass emigration was an enormously lucrative enterprise fully exploited. Few immigrants could afford to travel in first or second class: Most purchased the much cheaper berths in steerage, the name given to both an area of a ship and to the hordes of passengers crowded there. Steerage was simply a below-deck compartment near the ship's steering equipment, a cargo hold not particularly well-suited to human cargo. To maximize profits, owners of the larger ships would sometimes cram as many as two thousand passengers into steerage. They slept in rows of bunks. Draped blankets separated men from women. Ventilation was poor, non-existent during storms when the few hatches had to be kept closed. The stench was unbearable.

Robert Louis Stevenson in Steerage

On a trip from Scotland to the United States in the 1870s, famous writer Robert Louis Stevenson, author of *Treasure Island*, spent much of his time exploring the steerage compartments and socializing with its passengers, although he himself had a second class cabin. Stevenson wrote of his experiences in *The Amateur Emigrant*:

When Jones and I entered we found a little company of our acquaintances seated together at the triangular foremost table. A more forlorn party, in more dismal circumstances, it would be hard to imagine. The motion here in the ship's nose was very violent; the uproar of the sea often overpoweringly loud. The yellow flicker of the lantern spun round and round and tossed the shadows in masses. The air was hot, but it struck a chill from its foetor. From all around in the dark bunks, the scarcely human noises of the sick joined into a kind of farmyard chorus. . . . Singing was their refuge from discomfortable thoughts and sensations. One piped in feeble tones, "O why I left my hame?" which seemed a pertinent question in the circumstances. Another, from the invisible horrors of a pen where he lay dog-sick upon the upper shelf, found courage, in a blink of his sufferings, to give us several verses of the 'Death of Nelson'; and it was odd and eerie to hear the chorus breathe feebly from all sorts of dark corners, and "this day has done his dooty" rise and fall to be taken up again in this dim inferno, to an accompaniment of plunging, hollow-sounding bows and the rattling spray-showers overhead. (It seemed to me the singer, at least, that day had done his duty. For to sing in such a place and in such a state of health is cheerfully heroic. Like a modern Theseus, he thus combated bad air, disease and darkness, and threw aboard among his fellows some pleasant and courageous thoughts.

ABOVE: *The steerage deck of the S.S. Patricia, circa 1890. Good weather produced happy scenes such as this, but in bad weather, passengers were cramped in foul conditions below deck.*

Advertisements had promised plentiful food, but in reality it was often scarce and invariably of poor quality. The luckier, or better informed, passengers brought their own baskets of sausages and loaves, traditional foods that nourished and comforted them. For some, of course, the question of food was moot; seasickness had rendered them incapable of eating.

It is no wonder that the crowds debarking at Ellis Island resembled "huddled masses." Physically weakened and sick with worry, the steerage passengers had just endured the additional humiliation of watching the first and second class passengers dropped off directly in Manhattan, where a perfunctory inspection and a swift admittance awaited them. Steerage passengers were then typically loaded onto ferries and barges and taken to Ellis Island. In the peak years of the early twentieth century, as many as seven thousand immigrants might be processed in a single day. Thousands more might spend the day, or several days, waiting on the ferries. In a journey marked

by epic delays, this was the most excruciating wait of all, endured as it was in clear sight of Ellis Island, the Statue of Liberty, and Manhattan. If comforts and amenities had been minimal on the steamships, they were non-existent on the ferries: no seats, no food, no water. Worst of all, there was no forward movement, no progress. Time spent waiting was time spent worrying.

At the Island

What kind of experience an immigrant would have at Ellis Island depended largely on what year he or she entered. As the years advanced, physical conditions generally improved due to the efforts of several humanitarian commissioners and, at one point, the intervention of none other than Teddy Roosevelt. Over time, benches were added in the long, sectioned lines in the registry room. Money

ABOVE: *The refurbished Great Hall, site of the inspection process, as it appears today. In its active years, the open space of the Great Hall was divided by iron railings into aisles and holding pens, and to many immigrants and workers it looked more like a prison than the entrance to the land of the free.*

exchangers were regulated carefully to protect immigrants unfamiliar with currency and exchange rates. Recreation facilities were added for the benefit of children and long-term detainees. Food services were improved. But another kind of change marked the passing years as well, one far less congenial to the immigrants: Admission standards and inspection procedures grew progressively more demanding and restricting, reflecting the larger change in American public opinion on the immigration issue. Immigrants in later years would need to demonstrate adequate financial resources ($25 was informally considered the minimum), pass literacy tests as of 1917, and, after World War I, endure a litany of questions regarding political allegiances and affiliations. In short, as the treatment and processing of immigrants became more humane and efficient, the gateway to America itself was gradually but inevitably closing.

BELOW: *Genuine artifacts on display today in the main building baggage room. Immigrants would store their crates and baskets here while they proceeded to the registry room.*

ABOVE: *A Slavic mother and child at Ellis Island in 1905. The woman in the background wears her new identification tags as she carries her baggage in the traditional peasant manner.*

Following the manifests, lists of names compiled on board the ships, the immigrants debarked thirty at a time in groups that would stay together throughout the inspection process except for those marked for detention or additional examinations. Passing under the canopy at the front entrance, the passengers made their way into the large first floor baggage room, where their heavier belongings could be ticketed and stored until the ordeal was over and their destiny known. Immigrants parted with their possessions reluctantly; stolen, lost, and damaged goods were not unheard of. Many preferred to carry as much as possible on their bodies—money hung in pouches around their necks, significant family keepsakes stored in pockets. This preference, along with the common practice of wearing multiple layers of clothing regardless of the season, accounts for the puffy, shapeless look of immigrants in many old photographs. The more they could wear, the less they had to carry.

A slow climb up the crowded stairs led the immigrants from the baggage room to the registry room, the high, vaulted-ceilinged chamber better known as the Great Hall. At the top of the stairs, uniformed officials surveyed the procession. Guards stamped identification cards and steered the immigrants into the aisles, which formed a maze of iron railings. The iron bars existed to regulate movement in

When we were getting off of Ellis Island, we had all sorts of tags on us. Now that I think of it, we must have looked like marked-down merchandise in Gimbel's basement store or something. 'Where are you going, who's waiting for you?' and all that. Then we were put in groups, and our group was going to the Erie Railroad Station in New Jersey.

—Ann Vida, Hungarian Immigrant in 1921, interviewed in 1986.

LEFT: *Stairs leading from the baggage room to the Great Hall registry room. In the peak years of immigration, the inspection process would begin as the immigrants ascended these crowded stairs. From the top, doctors would survey the new arrivals and begin sorting out those who appeared infirm.*

Papa had been notified . . . to come to New York. I have a vivid memory of seeing him holding us by the hands through an iron fence. He was not permitted in the same room with us. With tears running down his cheeks, he asked me to take care of the children as best I could.

—*Martha Knaupp Kohlroser, German immigrant in 1927, from a 1985 letter.*

ABOVE: *The Great Hall during the peak years of immigration. Some of the areas sectioned off by railings were the lines to the inspectors' booths; others were reserved for those awaiting further medical or mental examinations. Before benches were installed in the early 1900s, immigrants had to stand or sit on the floor.*

the Great Hall but created the impression of a prison, an impression that lasted in the memories of even those immigrants who passed through quickly and without incident. Immigrants marked for detention would be held in cage-like configurations of iron railings just outside of the main inspection lines. Tensions ran high in the Great Hall, arising both from the fearful and confused immigrants and from the overworked staff. Uncontrollable crying was common and contagious.

Those not detained for medical reasons proceeded one at a time to the front of the registry room where an interview with the primary inspectors awaited. With interpreters on hand to assist, the inspectors asked a series of twenty-nine standard questions concerning personal history, identification, marital status, and prospective employment. Beginning in the early 1900s, most of these questions were asked on board the ships and the basic information included on the manifests. Most questions were simple; some, however, could be trickier than they

ABOVE: *When possible, immigrants brought with them the fruits of their cultures, such as this elaborate zither. Music could provide relief and solace during the long hours of waiting.*

LEFT: *Many immigrants brought traditional clothing with them, but, once inside, learned to dress as Americans to avoid being easy targets.*

appeared. If, for, example, an immigrant were asked if he or she already had employment secured in America, the correct answer was no. The Alien Contract Labor Law of 1885 prohibited such pre-arrangements. Immigrants, eager to assure the inspector that they would not become public charges, might be tempted to answer yes, even if it were a lie. In cases like this, immigrants were detained until it became clear whether they had already lined up employment in America.

[Two-year old] Walter took sick and was admitted to the hospital. He was there six weeks and died on February 9, 1921. We were confined on Ellis Island those six weeks. Our days were very long days and only one of us could go visit our sick boy for five minutes, once a week. We had to put on a gown as we were not allowed close to him. . . . Our boy died at ten minutes after 11:00 p.m. and we had to spend the night there. After all these years the picture in my mind is so clear when they took him down the hall wrapped in a sheet.

—*Martha Strahm, a Swiss immigrant in 1920, interviewed in 1988.*

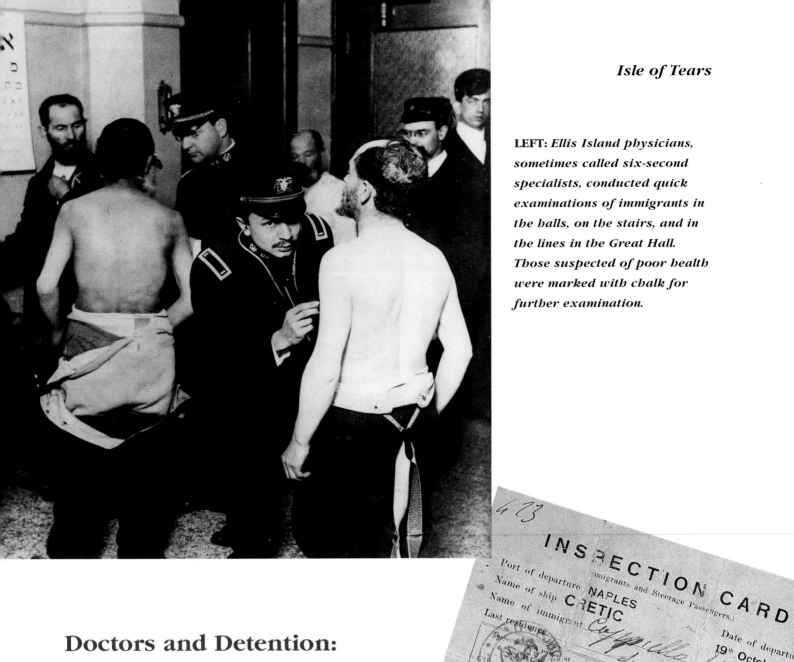

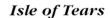

LEFT: *Ellis Island physicians, sometimes called six-second specialists, conducted quick examinations of immigrants in the halls, on the stairs, and in the lines in the Great Hall. Those suspected of poor health were marked with chalk for further examination.*

Doctors and Detention: Trouble at the Gate

The long, slow moving lines in the Great Hall afforded doctors the opportunity to perform cursory examinations as the immigrants waited to meet with inspectors. They were concerned primarily with "loathsome contagious diseases" but would make note of any condition that might prohibit immigrants from supporting themselves once inside the gate. The fast-working doctors inspected scalps and fingernails, listened to breathing, thumped chests, and, in the most feared examination of all, lifted eyelids either with their fingers or with a buttonhook-like device to check for indications of trachoma, a highly contagious eye disease that was common in

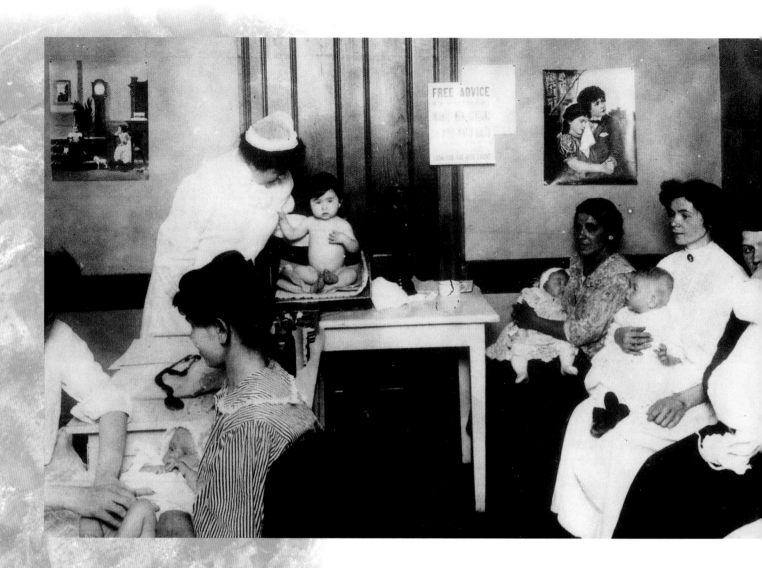

Everybody is nervous when you go through that doctor. Because it's the fear that you don't know what you have in your eyes. What could they find? But after you pass, it's a great joy and a great relief in your mind and heart.

—Rose Breci, an Italian immigrant who passed through Ellis Island in 1911.

Europe and virtually unknown in America. Then incurable, trachoma meant likely blindness and certain rejection.

Doctors indicated any evidence of debilitating or contagious physical conditions with chalk marks on the immigrants' clothing: E for eyes, Sc for scalp, and so on. Those with chalk marks were led from the registry line and put in detention "cages" until a more thorough medical examination could be performed. Those immigrants familiar with English might be able to decode the chalk

LEFT: *Nurses assist the mothers of infants in the main building changing room. Many infants contracted contagious illnesses or took ill during the journey and had to be moved to the hospital.*

BELOW: *An inspector examines an immigrant woman's papers. The indecipherable chalk marks on her clothing indicate some reason for further examination or detention.*

marks and either confirm or assuage their fears. But those marked with the cryptic X would be taken on a different route. X meant that doctors had reason to suspect mental problems, retardation or insanity. These immigrants were removed to a separate testing room and asked to complete simple analytical tasks such as fitting pegs into holes. Language and cultural differences could easily be misconstrued as signs of mental weakness or derangement. Fortunately, the Ellis Island mental specialists, among them the well-known Dr. Knox, were enlightened enough to understand the likelihood of faulty diagnosis. Only a tiny percentage of immigrants were ever rejected for "mental defects," but a tiny percentage of twelve million still amounted to thousands being judged unfit for mental reasons.

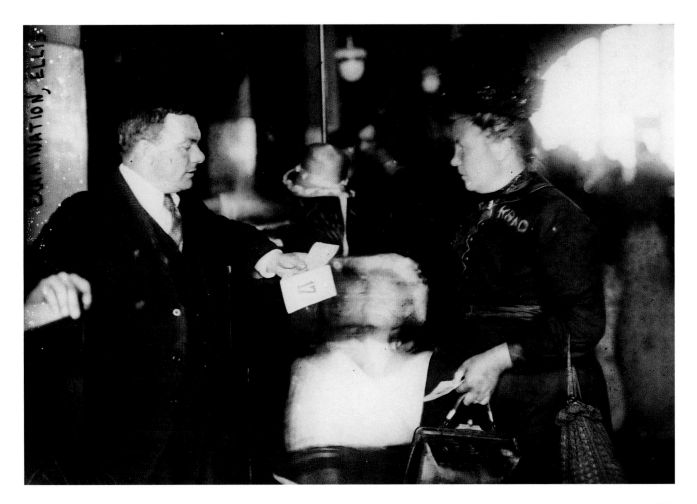

X is for Knox

Any immigrants marked with the letter X in chalk would be taken for mental testing. Before the arrival of Dr. Howard A. Knox, mental testing at Ellis Island had meant an informal interview and some simple mathematical problems. Language and cultural differences often led to misunderstandings and mis-evaluations. Knox, Assistant Surgeon at Ellis Island from 1910 until 1916, developed a thorough and, to his mind, objective "psychotesting" procedure. Knox began with an interview, through which he established the immigrants' cultural and educational backgrounds. The immigrants were then required to complete written exams and analytical form-board puzzles. Using a complex formula, Knox or his associates would factor in variables and arrive at a numerical intelligence rating. After Knox's method was introduced at Ellis Island, insanity certifications rose greatly.

> The whole experience was very frightening . . . They brought me up to a room . . . they put a pegboard before me with shapes and little holes. . . . I had to put them in place, the round ones and the square ones . . . and I did it perfectly. They said, 'oh, we must have made a mistake. This little girl . . . naturally she doesn't know English, but she's very bright, intelligent.' So they took the cross [chalk mark] off me so we were cleared.

—Victoria Sarfatti Fernandez, a Macedonian Jewish immigrant in 1916, interviewed in 1985.

RIGHT: *This large English family posed for a portrait outside the front entrance in 1908, as immigration officers looked on.*

17~'08.

ABOVE: Emigrants being cleared for departure in Poland. After World War I, the United States Government required that most of the inspection and approval processes be conducted in the United States consulates overseas, to ease the flow of people on the island.

Immigrants were detained for many reasons beyond the medical and mental. Some criteria, the more objective and verifiable ones, held steady throughout the years. Others were more subjective and influenced by cultural bias and changes in social attitudes. Criminal records of any kind meant likely detention and deportation, as did demonstrated anarchistic or communist affiliations. Women traveling alone and without sponsors or family already in America were almost always detained for fear that they might be lured into prostitution. The majority of detained immigrants would go before a Special Inquiry Board with offices on-site at Ellis Island. Their cases were heard separately by three Immigration Service officers. The time consuming board hearings turned some immigrants into residents of Ellis Island. For this purpose, the island had dormitories, laundry rooms, food services, and recreational facilities. In the post World War I years, the number of detained aliens would rise dramatically, as would the length of the average detention. Many immigrants recall Ellis Island not as their first stop but as their first home. For the deported, Ellis Island might be the only piece of America they would see.

It would happen sometimes that these interpreters—some of them—were really soft-hearted people and hated to see people being deported and they would, at times, help the aliens by interpreting in such a manner as to benefit the alien and not the government.
—*Edward Ferro, an Ellis Island interpreter,
1910-22, interviewed in 1968.*

Christmas at Ellis Island

Each December, immigrants detained at Ellis Island for medical or legal reasons were treated to a Christmas service. In the peak years of immigration, and later in the peak years of detention, this might mean up to 2,000 attendees. Presents provided by various Christian and charitable organizations were heaped on a long table— white bags for women, brown for men. Men received socks, a handkerchief, fruit, and cigars. Women received the same except for stockings in place of the socks and cigars. Children were offered cake and a toy. All received a bar of soap, and, according to observers, many detainees tried to eat the soap, thinking it was candy. Services were delivered in several languages. Detainees sang Christmas songs around a huge tree and sat down to one of the better meals they were likely to have during their stay at Ellis Island.

In 1905, Commissioner Robert Watchorn presided over the Christmas ceremony. The meal featured bean soup, turkey, baked ham, succotash, mince pie, and tea and coffee. With the aim of introducing the immigrants to the values they would be expected to adopt once in America, Commissioner Watchorn concluded the ceremony by leading the singing of "My Country 'tis of Thee."

ABOVE: *Each year, the Ellis Island staff offered a Christmas ceremony and meal for detainees. Immigrants received modest gifts and were treated to a rare feast of turkey, succotash, and pie.*

Christmas Festival
ELLIS ISLAND
Saturday, December 24th, 1932
at 2 P.M.
CONCERT 2 to 3 P.M.
Miss Lucrezia Bori, Signor Giovanni Martinelli
and N. B. C. Symphony Orchestra
———
INTERNATIONAL BROADCAST
by courtesy of
National Broadcasting Company, New York and
Reichs Rundfunk Gesselschaft, Berlin
Admission by Ticket Only
Boat for Ellis Island leaves Barge Office promptly at 12:45 and 1:30 P.M.

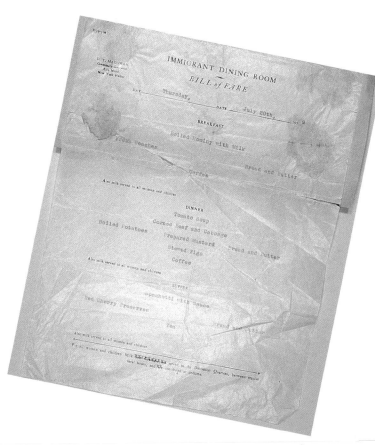

BELOW: *A group of Germans eating lunch in 1926. Fare at Ellis Island was generally bland and ordinary, but it was here that many Immigrants had their first taste of American favorites such as bananas and ice cream.*

Getting Off the Island

If all went smoothly with the inspector, and in most cases it did, final approval followed. They had made it. It was cause for quiet and sometimes not so quiet celebration. Certainly, the burden was lifted and the immigrants could now freely breathe the air of their new country, but by no means did this signal the end of the ordeal. Getting off Ellis Island, locating relatives, and arranging travel to final destinations could be difficult and dangerous in their own right. Money could be exchanged on Ellis Island and, after 1904, railroad tickets could be bought there, but once the immigrants, sometimes called "greenhorns," set foot on American soil, wearing their traditional clothing and speaking their native languages, the elation of arrival gave way to the reality of culture shock. Many would struggle to find living arrangements, suffer crippling isolation, and find themselves the victims of exploitative employers and opportunistic criminals.

LEFT: *In the long lines that led to the baggage room, even small children pulled their weight. Immigrants commonly wore as many layers of clothing as possible, regardless of season.*

RIGHT: *After the long processing ordeal was over, immigrants had to wait in line for rail tickets to their final destinations. Most signs at Ellis Island were written in five or six different languages.*

Fortunately, they were not alone. Social welfare organizations of all kinds worked tirelessly to protect and support the new immigrants. Such organizations as the Polish Society, the Italian Welfare League, the Hebrew Immigrant Aid Society, and the Catholic Welfare Council served and represented particular nationalities and religions. Others such as the Travelers' Aid Society and the Immigrants' Protective League offered their services to any immigrant in need. These groups fed and clothed immigrants, helped them find housing and employment, and often worked on behalf of those detained on Ellis Island. If Ellis Island treated the immigrants rather like cattle, a frequent and not entirely justified criticism, it can hardly be faulted given the sheer numbers of people it dealt with daily. Immigrant welfare organizations went a long way to humanize the process and introduce the new Americans to a supportive community.

This was the general experience at Ellis Island, a basic pattern upon which there were countless variations, one for each unique story. Twenty percent of the immigrants were detained for some reason. Approximately two percent were deported. During peak years, this two percent totaled nearly one thousand deportees a month, one thousand broken dreams and grim futures. Dr. Bruce T. Anderson, a U.S. Public Health Service physician at Ellis Island from 1919 to 1922, recalled how Ellis Island was a place of great emotional extremes, not only for the

LEFT: *This Italian mother and child sit outside a detention cell in 1905. Perhaps they were waiting for a detained family member; perhaps they just needed a rest.*

RIGHT: *A Russian Jew arrives at Ellis Island in 1905, during the heyday of Eastern European immigration. At home, Russian Jews were victimized by wars, poverty, and pogroms. They came to America in great numbers, settling in New York's Lower East Side, among other places.*

A Slavic immigrant, 1905. Although dormitories were built on Ellis Island to accommodate overnight and long-term detention, often the number of immigrants arriving was too great and some had to sleep on benches or the floor.

immigrants but for all who witnessed or participated in the mass migration to America: "Ellis Island was a place of great happiness and great sorrow. The coming together of families that had been separated for years was marvelous to see. Unfortunately, times did occur when a family had to be separated because of deportation or death. Then you wished you were somewhere else."

The Gateway Closes

CHAPTER THREE

The rebuilt main building
opened in 1900, three years after
the original wooden structure
was destroyed by fire. Pictured
here in 1905, the new structure
proved to be a durable and efficient facility throughout the
next fifty years of immigration.

LEFT: *The Statue of Liberty as viewed from the lawn at Ellis Island. For immigrants detained at Ellis Island and awaiting judgment, the always-visible statue must have been a painful reminder of their uncertain futures.*

RIGHT: *With their basket and bags behind them, this family stands on the Ellis Island ferry dock and looks out into New York Harbor.*

In the early morning of July 30, 1916, German saboteurs set fire to a munitions depot on the Black Tom Wharf in New Jersey. The awesome initial explosion and the smaller blasts that followed for almost three hours shattered windows and damaged buildings on nearby Ellis Island. During the ensuing panic and evacuations, some immigrants detained for mental examinations were reported to have cheered the explosions as if they were a fireworks display. As was the case with the fire of 1897, none of the several hundred detainees and employees on the island at the time was seriously injured. Damage to the island facilities was repaired at a cost of $400,000.

The United States was on the verge of entering World War I. The Black Tom Wharf incident drove home the threat of war—a threat from the inside as well as from the outside—and influenced American opinion on immigration. Perhaps the United States had been too lenient and too generous. Perhaps it was time to close the gate. Thus, with a few broken windows and collapsed roofs, the decline of Ellis Island began. Successive twentieth century calamities—World War I, the Red Scare, the Great Depression—brought about xenophobia, increased demand for immigration quotas, and, ultimately, a reversal in the purpose and function of Ellis Island. As suspected anarchists, illegal aliens, and those immigrants who had not prospered and chose to return to Europe would discover, the gate swung both ways. Ellis Island, the workhorse of the American promise of sanctuary and opportunity, would soon detain, deport, and turn away immigrants, including some of the very people it had welcomed in earlier years.

LEFT: *In this 1926 portrait, a Lithuanian woman in a colorful shawl poses with her basket. As luggage was sometimes stolen or lost in handling, immigrants were especially protective of their belongings.*

RIGHT: *Those who made it through processing and became naturalized Americans took the citizenship oath in hearing rooms at Ellis Island.*

World War I

Before immigration quotas and the widespread fear of foreign-born anarchists, World War I had caused a sharp decline in immigration. Beginning in 1914 with the assassination of Archduke Francis Ferdinand in Sarajevo, the Great War turned prospective immigrants into soldiers or prisoners in their homes. In one year, immigration plummeted by nearly a million and continued to drop throughout the conflict. As Fort Gibson before it had done, the relatively quiet Ellis Island prepared for a wartime role.

Although the United States did not enter the war until 1917, the international conflict created special problems and necessitated new procedures at Ellis Island

Ellis Island
Commissioners of Note

In its sixty-two years of operation, Ellis Island was governed by twelve different commissioners of immigration in New York, from Colonel John B. Weber to Rudolf Reimer. Many commissioners were already well-known and influential public figures at the time of their appointment. Many were authors, politicians, and statesmen. Here is a list of the most notable among them.

Colonel John B. Weber: 1890–1893

Weber was a Civil War colonel, a political opponent of Grover Cleveland, a Republican congressman, and commissioner-general of the 1901 Pan-American Exposition in Buffalo, New York, his hometown. He published his memoirs, *The Autobiography of John B. Weber*, in 1924.

Dr. Joseph Henry Senner: 1893–1902.

Weber's successor, Dr. Senner was an Austrian native who attended the University of Vienna and, after graduating, pursued a career as a lawyer and a journalist. Before and after his stint as commissioner, Senner was a successful publisher of such newspapers and journals as the *Milwaukee Herald* and the *National Provisioner*.

William Williams, Esq.: 1902–1905, 1909–1913

A Connecticut native, Williams was a direct descendent of William Williams, a signer of the Declaration of Independence. Williams was a successful lawyer with a degree from Harvard, a junior member of President Benjamin Harrison's cabinet, and a veteran of the Spanish-American War. Williams ran a Wall Street law firm until President Theodore Roosevelt recruited him to fight corruption at Ellis Island, which he did with great success.

Robert Watchorn: 1905–1909

A native of England, Watchorn entered the public realm via the coal workers' unions. He began as a coal worker himself, was elected president of the Pittsburgh District Miner's Union, and, years after his tenure on Ellis Island, became vice president of the Union Oil Company. He published his memoirs in 1958.

Frederic C. Howe: 1914–1919

Howe was a noted reformer, a city councilman in Cleveland, and an Ohio state senator. He was also the author of many books, including *The City: Hope and Democracy, Revolution and Democracy*, and *Confessions of a Reformer.*

Edward Corsi: 1931–1934

Son of a member of the Italian Parliament, Corsi immigrated to the United States in 1907, passing through Ellis Island during the peak year of twentieth century immigration. Corsi was a lawyer, journalist, and public servant in the United States, Italy, and Mexico. He ran unsuccessfully for the U.S. Senate in 1938. He was the Republican candidate for Mayor of New York in 1952, but was defeated by Robert Wagner. Before his death in 1965, Corsi was director of the New York World's Fair.

ABOVE: *Boats lined up at the ferry slip with Island 2 in the background.*

from the outset. Many of those slated for deportation had to be detained indefinitely because it was unsafe and illegal to ship them to war-torn European port cities. The Ellis Island dormitories and facilities were not designed for long-term detention, not, at least, until the 1914 appointment of Commissioner Frederic C. Howe, a former senator from Ohio and a well known municipal reformer. Howe felt strongly that long-term detainees should not be treated as prisoners. In his first few years as commissioner, he built recreation areas and handball courts, instituted adult classes and a kindergarten, and began a series of Sunday concerts and films at Ellis Island.

More than just a humanitarian, Howe was something of a social theorist. He believed that environment determines character, that problems such as crime and vice are attributable to inadequate social conditions. To the dismay of many public officials, Ellis Island became his proving ground. Ultimately, Howe would extend his generosity and humane treatment to national enemies. After the United States entered the war, the passengers of seized German and Austrian ships were interned on Ellis Island, joining there many of their immigrant countrymen who were being detained as suspected spies.

LEFT: *Immigrants entertaining themselves with music and dancing. The overhead sign reads, "No charge for meals here" in six different lan-*

BELOW: *World War I and the Red Scare led to frequent deportation of aliens. Here, German immigrants arrive at Hoboken, New Jersey en route to Ellis Island for deportation.*

Because of its location, Ellis Island proved to be useful to both the army and the navy in the war effort. In 1918, the military took over the hospital and dormitories. Many detainees and sick immigrants were sent to quarters in New York and Philadelphia to make room for wounded servicemen. At the close of the war, Ellis Island prepared to resume receiving immigrants. As a result of the war, however, the immigration restrictionist movement in America had gained considerable popular and governmental support. In Europe, immigrants would once again flock to the ports in hopes of a new life in America, but fewer, many fewer than before, would ever reach American soil.

The Great Debate

The New Immigration . . . contained a large and increasing number of the weak, the broken and the mentally crippled of all races drawn from the lowest stratum of the Mediterranean basin and the Balkans, together with hordes of the wretched, submerged populations of the Polish Ghettos. Our jails, insane asylums and almshouses are filled with this human flotsam and the whole tone of American life, social, moral and political has been lowered and vulgarized by them.
—*Madison Grant,* **The Passing of the Great Race,** *C. Scribner's Sons, 1916.*

I welcome this tide of Immigration, because I believe there is nothing that can enter our ports so valuable to us as a pair of human hands eager and anxious to engage in labor upon our soil, to increase the volume of commodities available for you and me, to widen the field of production in which highly paid American laborers can find employment.
—*Representative Bourke Cochran of New York, speech to Congress, January, 1908.*

Quotas: The Beginning of the End

World War I, the Russian Revolution, and the ensuing Red Scare in America hardly marked the beginning of the immigration restrictionist argument. It had been raging for years, with proponents such as William Williams and Robert Watchorn, both former commissioners at Ellis Island. The principal arguments used by restrictionists had usually been practical in nature. They wanted to regulate and pace the assimilation of immigrants into America. They wanted to make sure that America, and especially the American

LEFT: *This Russian family is gathered by the windows in the Great Hall in 1905. Because of the mother's smile and the halo-like lighting effect, one author dubbed this photograph "Mona Lisa Visits Ellis Island."*

BELOW: *The dormer windows in the east side of the Great Hall look out on the towering Manhattan skyline. A great many new Americans settled in New York City, where many ethnic enclaves continue to thrive today.*

work force, could absorb the immigrants without disturbing the quality of life and jobs available to established citizens.

In the post-World War I years, however, a new, more virulent strain of anti-immigration sentiment gained momentum. Political and racial arguments came to the fore of the immigration restrictionist movement. Anarchistic or communist leanings became a common reason for deportation. In addition, many Americans disliked the predominance of southern and eastern European immigrants, and immigration policy would eventually reflect this sentiment. For the immigrants, the

LEFT: *Driven by the desire to reach America, this young Finnish man arrived at Ellis Island as a stowaway in 1926. Once there, he no doubt faced a more-than-usual amount of interrogation at a special inquiry board hearing.*

post-war environment was one of suspicion, scrutiny, and, often, overt racism. Still, this atmosphere alone could not deter the wave of immigrants. In 1920 and 1921, after the wartime slump, immigration numbers rose to rival those of the peak years of the early twentieth century. For the beleaguered Ellis Island staff, still depleted from the war years, this must have seemed like a return to business as usual. In actuality, it was the last great flame of immigration, quickly extinguished by sweeping changes in U.S. immigration policy.

The Russian Revolution of 1917 heightened America's fear of communists and anarchists. All radicals, including the American-born, were subject to harassment and arrest, but the period was especially difficult for suspected subversives who were foreign-born. New immigration laws passed in 1918 had broadened the grounds for deportation to include the mere possession of anarchist literature. The Palmer raids of 1919 and 1920, named after the zealously anti-Communist Attorney General A. Mitchell Palmer, targeted for deportation alien members of labor organizations. Many were sent to Ellis Island to await deportation. Among those detained was Emma Goldman, the famous Russian-born anarchist who had arrived in America at Castle Garden in 1885 and left from Ellis Island, along with 249 deported aliens, in 1919. In the same

LEFT: *An American flag displayed on the side wall of the Great Hall. Despite the difficulties of processing, most immigrants had strong patriotic feelings about their new nation.*

BELOW: *In this hearing room, Ellis Island detainees would go before a board of special inquiry to determine whether they would be admitted or deported. Reasons for deportation ranged from medical to political.*

year, Commissioner Howe, aghast at the imprisonment and deportation of aliens without proper hearings, bitterly resigned.

Immigration quotas officially went into effect in 1921 when President Warren G. Harding signed a temporary emergency act that had been previously vetoed by Woodrow Wilson. The first quota allowed from each country three percent of the number of people from that country already living in the United States according to the census of 1910. One of the intended effects of the quota was to

dramatically reduce the number of southern and eastern Europeans allowed in and to favor the northern and western Europeans. As a temporary emergency act, the first quota had to be re-approved each year. The Immigration Act of 1924 reduced the annual national quota to two percent and turned quotas into permanent law. In determining what two percent actually meant in numbers, the 1890 census was used—a census taken well before the great influx of "new" immigrants.

The new laws created havoc and hysteria in Europe. Annual quotas began on July 1 and ended on June 30. No more than ten percent of the quota could be filled in a single month, so hopeful immigrants would have to arrive early in the month, creating competition among immigrants and a kind of race among steamship companies. This dangerous practice was terminated when the United States moved the inspection and admission process abroad, to U.S. consulates in European cities. After that, all immi-

LEFT: *Island 2, here seen from Island 1, was created from subway excavation landfill in 1898. It was the site of the hospital and the laundry building.*

grants boarding ships to America already had to have approved visas. On Ellis Island, this meant the virtual end of immigration traffic, or at least the beginning of the end.

The Great Depression, World War II, and the End of an Era

The Great Depression of the 1930s, as it turned out, did as much to dissuade immigrants as all the restrictionist legislation of the 1920s. In an ironic turn, many immigrants already in the country chose to leave, discouraged by diminishing opportunity and increasing hostility to outsiders. Unable to afford ship fare, some converted to anarchism, or made a show of it, to convince officials of their revolutionary intentions and to earn a free passage home. Many of these "unwanteds," following the practice established in the 1920s, were deported from Ellis Island and endured, once again, the horrors of the ocean passage in steerage. In 1932, aliens leaving the country outnumbered those coming in, a balance that would persist throughout the decade.

ABOVE: *Many immigrants, even those who were admitted swiftly, recalled Ellis Island as a prison of iron bars and cages.*

Ellis Island had become essentially a detention and deportation center, the last stop on the way out rather than the first on the way in. In the years after Commissioner Howe's resignation, conditions and staff morale deteriorated. Detainees often lived in lice-ridden squalor with little opportunity for exercise or recreation. Accusations of employee corruption, echoes of the old Castle Garden days, resurfaced. Into this mess, President Herbert Hoover sent his newly appointed commissioner of Ellis Island, Edward Corsi, who himself had immigrated through Ellis Island from Italy in 1907. Corsi sought to reestablish the civil and humane spirit of the Howe years, re-instituting some of Howe's policies and adding many of his own.

ABOVE: *Reformist photojournalist Jacob Riis captured this scene of children and their parents at play at the Ellis Island roof garden. As the years progressed, recreational facilities for families and detainees greatly improved.*

RIGHT: *Children were a favorite subject of photographers who visited Ellis Island, Here, an Italian boy in an ornate military costume poses on the dock.*

Excerpt from the Alien Anarchist Act of 1918-20

. . . the following aliens shall be excluded from admission to the United States:

(a) Aliens who are anarchists;

(b) Aliens who advise, advocate, or teach, or who are members of or affiliated with any organization, association, society, or group that advises, advocates, or teaches, opposition to all organized government;

(c) Aliens who believe in, advise, advocate, or teach. . . :(I) the overthrow by force or violence of the Government of the United States or of all forms of law, or (2) the duty, necessity, or propriety of the unlawful assaulting or killing of any officer or officers . . ., or (3) the unlawful damage, injury, or destruction of property, or (4) sabotage;

(d) Aliens who write, publish, or cause to be written or published, or who knowingly circulate, distribute, print, or display . . . any written or printed matter, advising, advocating, or teaching opposition to all organized government. . . .

(e) Aliens who are members of or affiliated with any organization . . . that writes, circulates, distributes, . . . or that has in its possession . . . any written or printed matter of the character described in subdivision (d).

ABOVE: *Many immigrants fought as Americans during World War I, to protect the nations they had left behind and still held dear. Displays at Ellis Island today commemorate the role of new Americans from a multitude of ethnic and cultural backgrounds who came together to fight.*

RIGHT: *In post World War I America, immigration became a hotly debated issue. Songs such as this one preached the virtues of tolerance and patriotism.*

Corsi bolstered moral with recreational activities, opened the door for visitors, and allowed detainees to use telephones. These modest improvements reflected Corsi's commitment to a habitable and sympathetic environment. He was determined to treat detainees not as prisoners but as victims of the vagaries of politics and economics, unfortunate losers of the immigration gamble. Corsi resigned in 1934 but left a substantial list of recommendations with the new Franklin D. Roosevelt administration. Many of his ideas were put into effect by the New Dealers. New buildings, ferry slips, and landscaping altered the appearance of the island. As part of the Federal Art Project, out-of-work artists were hired to paint large murals in the dining room. Designed by painter Edward Laning, the murals depicted the struggles of immigrant workers in American factories.

World War II occasioned the last flurry of activity at Ellis Island. First, the threat of war in Europe spurred a brief rise in immigration numbers. In 1939, as America attempted to maintain neutrality, the United States Coast Guard began occupying several buildings on Ellis Island for use as training facilities. After the United States entered the war in 1941, Ellis Island once again served as a detention center for enemy aliens, and its hospitals were again devoted to the war effort. Finally, in an act markedly different than those that followed World War I, President Harry S. Truman signed the

Displaced Persons Act of 1948. This measure allowed a total of nearly 400,000 war-victimized Europeans into the country over a period of several years. A generous and humane exception to the rule, the Displaced Persons Act did not hold the gate open for long. A short time later, the McCarran-Walter Act, a potent and wide-ranging restrictionist law designed to protect the United States from communism, reduced immigration quotas to new lows.

From the time of the Immigration Act of 1924, Ellis Island's function as an immigrant receiving station had declined steadily. In 1943, in fact, all New York immigration operations except detention had been moved from Ellis Island to the Immigration and Naturalization Service (INS) headquarters at 70 Columbus Circle in Manhattan. Ellis Island began to look like a dinosaur, built in anticipation of the great wave of immigration but now too large and expensive. The size of the facility no longer matched the reduced scope of the enterprise. In 1953, INS Director Edward J. Shaughnessy visited the island and found a total of 237 detainees served by a staff of 250. With annual maintenance expenses of close to a million dollars, the closing of Ellis Island was inevitable.

LEFT: *A view of the restored rail office. The column with the gold plaque on it has come to be known as the kissing post because it was the site of so many joyous reunions between the newly admitted and their relatives already in America.*

RIGHT: *The stairs in the main building lead from the ground floor baggage room to the third floor offices.*

LEFT: *The New Ferry House, which is situated between Islands 1 and 2, was built in 1934–1935.*

ELLIS ISLAND

In over half a century of operation, Ellis Island had seen twelve different commissioners, myriad additions and modifications to its buildings and to the island itself, fires, explosions, and the faces of over twelve million immigrants from all around the world. On Friday, November 12, 1954, fifty-seven years after Annie Moore from County Cork was the first immigrant processed at the first federal immigrant receiving station, Ellis Island was unceremoniously closed. Arne Peterssen, a Norwegian sailor and the last detainee, was ferried from the island on the S.S. *Ellis Island* along with some records, furniture, and the remaining staff. Visitors to the Statue of Liberty in the coming years might wonder at the deteriorating French Renaissance main building on the overgrown, abandoned island, but Ellis Island would not open its gates again until the 1970s.

RIGHT: *These young Dutch children in traditional clogs are holding their official identification papers.*

United States Immigration Through the Port of New York: 1892-1954

Year	Total	Year	Total	Year	Total
1892	444,987	1913	892,653	1934	17,574
1893	343,422	1914	878,052	1935	23,173
1894	219,046	1915	178,416	1936	23,434
1895	190,928	1916	141,390	1937	31,644
1896	263,709	1917	129,446	1938	44,846
1897	180,556	1918	28,867	1939	62,035
1898	178,748	1919	16,731	1940	48,408
1899	242,573	1920	225,206	1941	23,622
1900	341,712	1921	560,971	1942	10,173
1901	388,931	1922	209,778	1943	1,089
1902	493,262	1923	295,473	1944	1,075
1903	631,835	1924	315,587	1945	2,636
1904	606,019	1925	137,492	1946	52,050
1905	788,219	1926	149,289	1947	83,884
1906	880,036	1927	165,510	1948	104,665
1907	1,004,756	1928	157,887	1949	113,050
1908	585,970	1929	158,238	1950	166,849
1909	580,617	1930	147,982	1951	142,903
1910	786,094	1931	63,392	1952	183,222
1911	637,003	1932	21,500	1953	87,483
1912	605,151	1933	12,944	1954	98,813

Source: Historic Research Study, Statue of Liberty/Ellis Island, by Harlan D. Unrah, U.S. Department of the Interior/National Park Service.

Immigrants often arrived at Ellis Island in the traditional clothing of their homelands and were advised to dress as inconspicuous Americans. Many would settle in ethnically concentrated areas, however, where the Old World traditions thrived again.

From Ruin to Restoration

CHAPTER FOUR

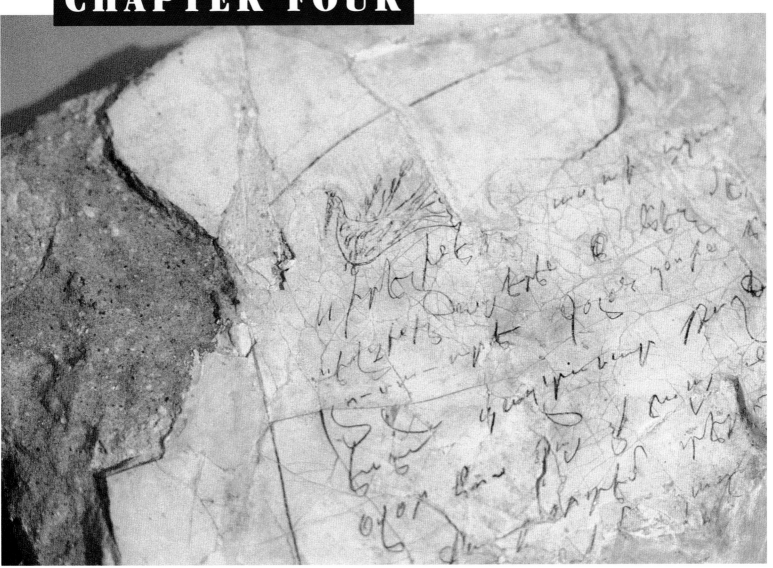

When the main building was prepared for restoration, workers uncovered years of multi-lingual graffiti on the walls.

The abandoned Ellis Island bore no resemblance to the Little Oyster Island of centuries before. Years of continued expansion had transformed the tiny three-acre sandbar into a three island complex covering twenty-seven acres. Over two dozen buildings stood neglected and deteriorating on the island once thought to be unsuitable for construction. Generations of artifacts, from turn-of-the-century kitchen equipment to multi-lingual graffiti carved in the stone walls, collected dust and plaster, the debris of detritus of a receding era.

LEFT: *Fort Clinton at New York City's Battery Park, looking at New York Harbor, Ellis Island, and, behind it, the New Jersey shore.*

BELOW: *An invitation to a "Farewell to Ellis Island" dinner party. In its sixty-two years of operation, Ellis Island employed thousands as immigration officers, doctors, maintenance workers, translators, food service workers, etc. New York City Mayor Fiorello LaGuardia was perhaps Ellis Island's most famous employee.*

In the years after its 1954 closing, however, Ellis Island would return to its virgin state in at least one respect; as had been the case in the early days of Dutch and English settlement, no one but the gulls knew exactly what to do with it. Over the next twenty years, proposals would flood in, schemes and designs ranging from the feasible to the bizarre. In each instance, some difficulty prohibited the development of the island; flaws were discovered, offers withdrawn, controversies ignited. The federal government put the island up for sale on several occasions. Interested developers came and went. Nothing happened.

Through nearly two decades of debate and indecision, one idea persisted—the notion that the proposed hotels, convention centers, and industrial sites were desecrations, that Ellis Island was a significant and essential historical landmark worthy of preservation and restoration. Due to public sentiment, the efforts of several high-minded individuals, and, perhaps, to chance, the preservationist argument ultimately prevailed. First came the designation of Ellis Island as a national landmark in 1965. A decade later, visitors were allowed to tour the ruins. Finally, after a massive fund-raising campaign, Ellis Island was restored and opened as a museum and education center. In 1990, Ellis Island once again opened its doors to the world.

ABOVE: *This aerial photograph of Ellis Island made during the restoration shows the unnaturally rigid outlines of the mostly man-made islands.*

RIGHT: *Ellis Island's offices were closed rather hastily, and some furniture and office machinery were simply left behind. This manual typewriter was one of many leftover artifacts found amidst the debris.*

Ellis Island in Limbo

The post-immigration station Ellis Island might have been an airstrip, a hotel, or a prison. It was advertised as an ideal spot for an oil storage depot, a warehouse, and a manufacturing center. After 1954, government officials and private investors dreamed up a grand variety of potential uses, but none came to fruition. Most plans were withdrawn or shot down because of economic and structural reasons. The cost of the island itself was small compared to the great sums required to demolish the existing structures or adapt them to new purposes. Those who would retain some or all of the original buildings would have to deal with the inefficiency and obsolescence of turn-of-the-century architecture. Any proposal would have to factor in the additional cost of operating and maintaining ferries. Few developers made formal overtures, and those who did found their problems exacerbated by public resistance.

ABOVE: *After closing in 1954, the facilities on Ellis Island deteriorated rapidly.*

Ellis Island on Film

Body of Iron, Soul of Fire, *26 minutes, American Express Company, 1972.*

A documentary about the history of the Statue of Liberty with a short segment on immigration and Ellis Island.

The Golden Door, *15 minutes, Hearst Metronews Corporation, 1972.*

Portrays the history of Ellis Island with historical footage and photographs.

The Huddled Masses, *45 minutes, BBC, 1967.*

The ninth installment of the "America" series narrated by Alistair Cooke concentrates on the great wave of twentieth century immigration and the assimilation of immigrants into New York City ghettos.

An Island Called Ellis, *50 minutes, NBC, 1967.*

A TV documentary narrated by Jose Ferrer tours the abandoned Ellis Island immigration station and recalls the great wave of immigration.

Gateway, *20th Century Fox, 1938.*

Directed by Alfred Werker and starring Don Ameche. The most famous of all Ellis Island films, *Gateway* is Hollywood's treatment of the Ellis Island experience, although it is first a foremost a love story. Portions of the film were shot on location at Ellis Island.

ABOVE: *This old wheelchair was found in the rubble of the Hospital Building. While the restored main building has been open to the public for several years, the structures on Islands 2 and 3, including the hospital, remain in limbo.*

The first proposals aimed to extend Ellis Island's function as a public facility. The New York State Department of Corrections thought that it might make a handsome prison. Other state authorities suggested that it might serve to house homeless men, delinquent boys, or alcoholics. New Jersey, the state to which Ellis Island is closest, also expressed interest in acquiring the island and turning it into a park and museum complex, an idea championed by New Jersey Senator James F. Murray, Jr. When offered the chance to buy the island, however, New Jersey balked at the prohibitive costs. The state of New York too found no proposals sufficiently enticing to purchase the island from the federal government.

RIGHT: *A helicopter lowers hand-crafted copper poles onto the Ellis Island main building cupola. The original copper domes and spires were decayed beyond repair, and were replaced during the restoration.*

Declaring it surplus government property, the General Services Administration decided to put Ellis Island up for sale at an auction for private developers in 1956. Before any serious offers were tendered, strong public sentiment in favor of preservation prompted President Dwight D. Eisenhower to suspend the auction after only a week. Throughout the next year, the government struggled with various preservation plans. All were met with the same verdict—economically impossible. When a museum was proposed, a rival group in the midst of planning an immigration museum at Liberty Island objected, claiming that the Statue of Liberty was the

ABOVE: *In the 1960s, architect Philip Johnson proposed that Ellis Island be allowed to deteriorate naturally. Broken windows and other hazards would be removed, but natural erosion and infestation would be allowed to continue.*

true symbol of the American promise. After a year of inaction and frustrated plans, the island was once again put up for sale in 1958.

Between 1958 and 1965, the ideas continued to flow in. The developer who came closest to realizing his ambitions was Sol G. Atlas, a New York builder and the highest bidder in the auction. Atlas proposed a multi-million dollar pleasure island. He planned to raze all the existing structures and build a hotel, a museum, tennis courts, an outdoor "sail-in" movie theater, and a marina. Meanwhile, in perhaps the most bizarre proposal of all, New York Congressman Paul A. Fino supported a plan

BELOW: *An abandoned and decaying corridor in the contagious disease ward of the Hospital Building on Island 2.*

that would turn Ellis Island into a national lottery center. Fino justified the plan by making an analogy between the lottery and the gambling spirit of the immigrants. The General Services Administration continued to reject all proposals and developers, including the ever-persistent Sol Atlas, who was the high bidder in 1958, '59, and '60. Perhaps their reluctance had less to do with money and more to do with the public outrage that seemed to accompany every commercial proposal, every plan that did not honor Ellis Island's historical significance.

ABOVE AND RIGHT: *When restoration workers began efforts on Ellis Island in 1980, they found rooms and hall-ways filled with chipped paint and plaster. Although much of the Great Hall has been restored, many rooms remain in a state of decay.*

In the 1960s, proposals for Ellis Island took an idealistic turn. Cooper Union art students designed a model for a nuclear energy research center. Pratt Institute held a competition for Ellis Island designs and a host of grand ideas followed: museums, trade centers, a "United Nations of Religion." Shortly before his death, the famous architect Frank Lloyd Wright began preliminary designs for a futuristic dream city. A group of prominent New York educators and intellectuals proposed a "college of the future" for the site. Once again, enthusiasm and idealism waned when the cold reality of funding set in. At every turn, complications and ambivalence intervened, buying time until America would recognize and protect Ellis Island as a national treasure with the power to teach and to remind.

ABOVE: *Images of decay: thirty years of indeci-sion and neglect turned Ellis Island into ruins.*

A National Monument

Invoking the Antiquities Act of 1906, President Lyndon B. Johnson declared Ellis Island to be a national monument on May 11, 1965. The new monument would be administratively attached to the Statue of Liberty National Monument and overseen by the National Park Service (NPS), a branch of the United States Department of the Interior. Owing much to the support of several senators, including Edmund Muskie of Maine and Jacob Javits of New York, the national monument designation ended once and for all the bidding war and the consideration of commercial uses. Still, it would be many years filled with more ill-fated proposals before a clear plan of action appeared.

Several months after the national monument designation, President Johnson approved a six million dollar budget for the development and restoration of Ellis Island. The New York architect Philip Johnson was tapped to design the project. As a main attraction, Johnson submitted plans for "The Wall of the Sixteen Million," an elaborate forerunner of the Wall of Honor in which plaques bearing the names of immigrants would adorn the walls of a giant, hollow tower. In place of a traditional restoration project, Johnson proposed that the main building be allowed to deteriorate in a controlled manner. Wood and window glass would be removed. The invasion of vines and weeds into the building would be allowed to continue unchecked. Under careful supervision, the main building would be cultivated into safe and structurally stabilized ruins.

ABOVE: *A typical wall during the restoration project, with restoration workers' marks and measurements.*

Johnson's plan was lauded and approved, but, with the escalation of the war in Vietnam, available funds quickly disappeared and the project was shelved along with the many that had preceded it. The National Park Service followed with a modest and affordable plan for preservation in 1968. They called for minor repairs of the main building roof and the restoration of the S.S. *Ellis Island* ferry. The roof repairs were completed, but before the ferry could be tended to, it sank, at Ellis Island, in August of 1968.

It would be several years before the Ellis Island National Monument emerged again as a topic of national concern. In the interim, the quiet island came to the public's attention twice, under unusual circumstances. In early 1970, a militant Native American group had taken over the island of Alcatraz in California to protest government neglect of Native American issues. Following suit, a New York Native American organization attempted a similar protest on Ellis Island several months later. The takeover never happened, however, as a boat carrying over thirty protesters broke down mid-voyage and was seized by the Coast Guard.

Island of the Famous

At Ellis Island, I was born again. Life for me began when I was ten years old.   —**Edward G. Robinson**

Of the millions who passed through Ellis Island, hundreds would go on to become famous Americans. This is only a partial list.

Name	Occupation	Country	Year
Irving Berlin *(1888–1989)*	Composer	Russia	1893
Knute Rockne *(1888–1931)*	Football Coach	Norway	1893
Al Jolson *(1886–1950)*	Singer/Actor	Lithuania	1894
Kahlil Gibran *(1883–1931)*	Writer	Lebanon	1895
Samuel Goldwyn *(1882–1974)*	Producer	Poland	1896
Charles Atlas *(1893–1972)*	Bodybuilder	Italy	1903
Frank Capra *(1897–1991)*	Director	Italy	1903
Edward G. Robinson *(1893–1973)*	Actor	Rumania	1903
Max Factor *(1872–1936)*	Cosmetician	Russia	1906
Bob Hope *(1903–)*	Actor	England	1908
Claudette Colbert *(1903–1996)*	Actress	France	1912
Rudolph Valentino *(1895–1926)*	Actor	Italy	1913
Xavier Cougat *(1900–1990)*	Musician	Spain/Cuba	1915
Marcus Garvey *(1887–1940)*	Ethnic Leader	Jamaica	1916
Bela Lugosi *(1882–1956)*	Actor	Hungary	1921
Issac Asimov *(1920–1992)*	Writer	Russia	1923

ABOVE: *The total cost of the Ellis Island restoration project reached $160 million, making it one of the most expensive restorations in history.*

A more successful symbolic flight to Ellis Island followed in July of 1970. Evading the Coast Guard, sixty-four members of the National Economic Growth and Reconstruction Organization (NEGRO) landed on Ellis Island and attempted to set up a model self-sufficient community there. NEGRO actually succeeded in getting a permit from the National Park Service to establish a rehabilitation center for drug addicts and convicts. Financially unable to sustain the project, NEGRO left Ellis Island after a short stay. Their permit was revoked in 1973. Ellis Island returned to the state in which it had spent most of the two decades after the closing of the immigration station. Suffering ever-worsening dilapidation, abandoned but for the daytime watchman and the occasional nocturnal vandal, Ellis Island awaited its rebirth as an indispensable and celebrated American landmark.

BELOW: *Through much of the 1980s, restoration efforts had surrounded both the Statue of Liberty and the Ellis Island main building with scaffolding and cranes. This photo shows a close-up of the replacement domes, with New York City in the background.*

America's Biggest Haunted House

During and after its years as an active immigration receiving station, Ellis Island has been the location of much alleged supernatural and paranormal activity. Ellis Island librarian Barry Moreno collects such stories. Here is a sampling of his work.

- At night, watchmen, maintenance workers, and janitors have reported frequent sightings of a weeping woman in white.
- Over the years there have been numerous reports of inexplicable cold spots inside the main building.
- According to some observers, dogs brought onto Ellis Island bark loudly and, apparently, at nothing.
- Body-less voices have been reported in the Great Hall and in the Recreation Hall.
- The S.S. Ellis Island ferry, which sank in 1968, is supposed to be haunted by the ghost of Charles Waldo, an Ellis Island inspector who died on September 9, 1913 when a railing on the ferry collapsed and he drowned in the harbor.
- There were, of course, many deaths on Ellis Island, including a reported 3,000 suicides. There was also an on-island morgue.
- Just to add to the mood, Moreno mentions that Bela Lugosi passed through Ellis Island in 1921. Mary Mallon, better known as Typhoid Mary, an Irish immigrant and unwitting spreader of deadly typhoid fever, came to America through Ellis Island in the 1890s.

1976—Ellis Island Opens its Doors: Returnees Tour the Ruins

Perhaps it was the approaching American Bicentennial that renewed public interest in Ellis Island. Perhaps it was the continued dedication of many to see the island restored to its rightful condition and made accessible again to all Americans. For whatever combination of reasons, Ellis Island's second renaissance began in the mid-1970s. Over a fourteen year span, it would grow in recognition and undergo a complete restoration. But advances were small at first.

In 1974, Dr. Peter Sammartino, Chancellor of Farleigh Dickinson University in New Jersey, formed the Restore Ellis Island Committee, whose purpose was to raise funds for Ellis Island's rehabilitation. The initial success of the committee's efforts led to a clean-up campaign on the island. The National Park Service's first task was to make sure that the main building was safe for visitors. The entire island was cleaned of its debris, and the ferry landing area was repaired to allow tourists to debark. These minor but essential repairs did little to alter the run down appearance of the facility. To painstakingly restore the main building would cost between $75 and $100 million, according to an NPS estimate. Sammartino's lobbying efforts had gathered $1.5 million, just enough to staff the island and complete only the most essential repairs.

When Ellis Island was officially reopened to the public on May 28, 1976, the first tourists, many of whom were aged veterans of the original Ellis Island experience, encountered a kind of ghost town of broken windows, trees and moss growing through cracked floors, and dust collecting on leftover furniture and equipment. Still, the visitors

came, arriving on the ferries that left six times daily from the Statue of Liberty except during winter months. Followi1ng the path of the immigrants, the visitors were led on a tour through the main building. In some rooms, old original furniture was displayed in a modest attempt to evoke the heyday of immigration. Soon, ferries from New Jersey's Liberty State Park were also stopping at Ellis Island.

For the original tourists, the Ellis Island site was most likely a brief side trip on their visit to the Statue of Liberty, but the growing popularity of the tour called attention to the island's disrepair. Perhaps those early visitors were fortunate in one respect. The Ellis Island they found told two stories: one of the drama of immigration, the other of the consequences of years of neglect. There is

ABOVE: *The abandoned third-floor offices in the main building are quiet reminders of the bustle of activity that must have occurred there during the height of immigration.*

LEFT: *The high vaulted ceiling of the Great Hall had yellowed with age, and required a careful cleaning.*

no doubt that the reopening of the island in the 1970s was instrumental in the forthcoming efforts to rehabilitate and restore its facilities. Now only money, the perennial obstacle, stood in the way.

Lee Iacocca's Fund-Raising Campaign Paves the Way

Before Ellis Island had become a national monument, Chrysler Corporation Chairman Lee Iacocca had been invited by some investors to support a real estate project on Ellis Island. Iacocca, whose parents had come through Ellis Island, angrily refused to participate in the commercialization of what he considered to be an impor-

ABOVE: *Ellis Island went through a number of renovations during its operative years, and restoration architects had to choose a particular historical point to which to restore the interior. Architects decided to restore the Great Hall to its 1924 condition, and as a result, partitions on and below the end balcony were removed..*

tant landmark. Years later, President Reagan's Interior Secretary James Watt recruited Iacocca to lead a public-private partnership to raise funds for a Statue of Liberty renovation effort. Iacocca seized the opportunity to suggest that Ellis Island be included in the plan. Thus was the Statue of Liberty-Ellis Island Centennial Commission formed in May of 1982 with Iacocca as its head.

Over the next eight years, The Statue of Liberty-Ellis Island Foundation, Inc., raised nearly $400 million for the joint restoration project. Large sums came from corporations, wealthy individuals, and charitable organizations. Towns and cities across the country were encouraged to sponsor their own fund-raising drives, often using the time-tested techniques of bake sales, auctions, and raffles. The Advertising Council donated millions of dollars worth of free advertising in all media. The total effect of the foundation's fund-raising was not only to amass the fortune necessary to complete restoration but to unite the country in the effort and, as Iacocca had originally intended, to draw much-deserved attention to Ellis Island.

BELOW: *The interior of the Recreation Hall, site of Christmas ceremonies, film showings, and evenings of music and dancing.*

The responsibility for soliciting and approving plans and overseeing the restoration project belonged to the National Park Service (NPS), working in cooperation with The Ellis Island-Statue of Liberty Foundation, Inc . In a 1982 General Management Plan, the NPS detailed their particular goals and overarching objectives. Under the NPS plan, the most significant buildings, located on the northern part of the island, would be preserved and restored, along with the artifacts they contained, to offer an accurate image of the immigration experience. These buildings would also serve as educational facilities. Tours and exhibits would recall the immigrants' journey in vivid particularity. Other exhibits would provide historical context, treating the entire history of U.S. immigration and addressing its affect on the nation. The NPS also stressed the archival function of the new facility. With its rich collection of artifacts, its library, and its oral history listening room, part of the restored Ellis Island would serve as a research center for scholars and historians.

LEFT: *Visitors at Ellis Island identify their ancestors' names on the Wall of Honor. A computer terminal inside the baggage room allows visitors to find the exact locations of names on the wall.*

The American Immigrant Wall of Honor®

The American Immigrant Wall of Honor,® a sprawling stainless steel outdoor wall engraved with the names of immigrants who came through Ellis Island, was begun in 1988. Bearing 200,000 names, the first wall opened with the Ellis Island Immigration Museum in 1990. For donations starting at $100 dollars, donors can have their ancestors' names added to the wall. When demand exceeded available space, the original wall was replaced with a new one in 1993, this time bearing over 420,000 names. Currently, the total is 500,000 names and growing. Championed by Lee Iacocca (Chairman Emeritus of The Statue of Liberty–Ellis Island Foundation), the Wall of Honor is 652 and one half feet long and four feet ten inches high with columns of names engraved on both sides. Famous Americans such as Jay Leno, Barbra Streisand, and Edward Kennedy are among those whose ancestors are honored on the wall.

In response to growing interest and demand, the Wall of Honor campaign was reopened in 1996. Funds raised this time will go toward the creation of The American Family Immigration History Center™, a genealogical research center and database that will contain all extant records of New York Harbor and Ellis Island arrivals from 1892-1924, in addition to a collection of personal and family archives. The new addition to the Wall of Honor will be unveiled in 1998, while the Immigration History Center is scheduled to open, at Ellis Island, in 1999. Those interested can receive more information by writing to The Statue of Liberty-Ellis Island Foundation, Inc., P.O. Box Ellis, New York, New York, 10163, by calling (212) 883-1986, or by visiting their website at: www.ellisisland.org.

The actual process of restoration, especially of the behemoth main building, would require a knowledge of antiquated architecture and a shrewd understanding of the fit between old buildings and modern facilities. The NPS hired two firms, each with its own specialty, to collaborate on the project. Beyer Blinder Belle of New York specialized in the preservation of historic sites. Anderson Notter Feingold of Boston had demonstrated expertise in modernizing the facilities of old buildings. Under the supervision of an NPS project director, the two firms began the restoration in the fall of 1983. What they found was a landmark in shambles, surrounded by fences and barbed wire, battered by the elements during its thirty years of disuse.

The Main Building Restored

As the main building had been the crux of the immigration experience, so would it be the focus of the restoration effort. Those rooms that had witnessed the most human drama—the baggage room and the Great Hall registry room among others—would be restored to their conditions at the height of immigration and would become the sites of the major exhibits. Other parts of the building would be devoted to administration and research facilities. Blending old and new, the restoration project resulted in a facility that is true to its heritage and well-equipped for the rigors of a modern tourist site.

Guastavino Tiles

As workers were refurbishing and restoring the Great Hall, they were amazed to discover the stability and durability of the tiles of the high vaulted ceiling. Raphael Guastavino and his son, immigrants from Spain, had developed a self-supporting terra-cotta vaulting system which was used in other New York City landmarks as well, including the Oyster Bar at Grand Central Station. When workers examined the ceiling tiles in 1986, they found that only seventeen of over 28,000 tiles needed to be replaced—a remarkable feat of durability considering the years of neglect.

ABOVE: *The original canopy that led from the ferry landing to the main building was torn down at the order of Immigration Commissioner Edward Corsi in the 1930s. This steel and glass main entrance canopy was built during the reconstruction in the 1980s, and is a modernized interpretation of the original canopy that sheltered immigrants as they disembarked.*

Well before the fine craft of historically accurate restoration could begin, workers had to contend with myriad structural problems. Unheated for thirty years, the building had to be dried, a process that took well over a year. Following that, the entire structure was reinforced and prepared for a makeover. Surrounded by a web of scaffolding, the exterior brick facade and fine limestone trim were cleaned and repaired, along with roof tiles and the majestic dormer windows. Helicopters were used to re-set the four brick and limestone towers. The original copper domes and spires atop the towers were long gone and had to be replaced with new hand-crafted ones. The original main entrance canopy had been torn down at the order of Commissioner Corsi in the 1930s. Workers installed a modern steel and glass interpretation of the original. In the 1940s, the main

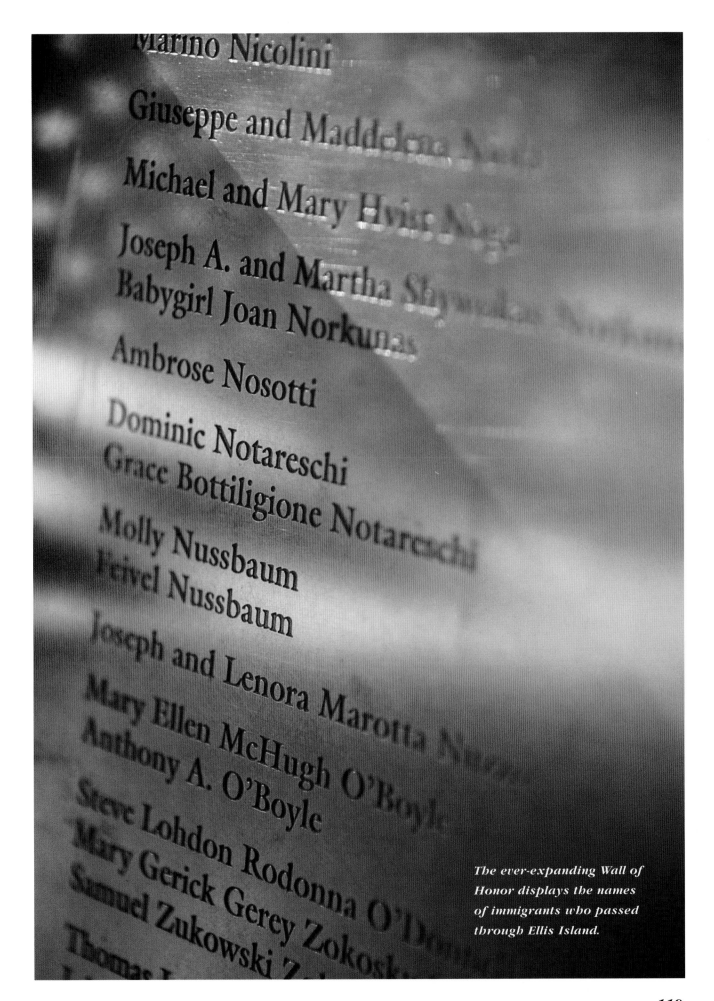

Marino Nicolini

Giuseppe and Maddalena Nadi

Michael and Mary Hritz Nagy

Joseph A. and Martha Shywed...

Babygirl Joan Norkunas

Ambrose Nosotti

Dominic Notareschi

Grace Bottiligione Notareschi

Molly Nussbaum

Feivel Nussbaum

Joseph and Lenora Marotta Nu...

Mary Ellen McHugh O'Boyle

Anthony A. O'Boyle

Steve Lohdon Rodonna O'D...

Mary Gerick Gerey Zokosk...

Samuel Zukowski Z...

Thomas...

The ever-expanding Wall of Honor displays the names of immigrants who passed through Ellis Island.

119

doors had been replaced with a row of windows. One of the final exterior projects was the restoration of the original entrance. From the ferry slip to the canopy to the main entrance into the baggage room, visitors at Ellis Island would follow the path of the immigrants, walk where they walked, see what they saw.

The centerpiece of the interior restoration was the Great Hall. As with every other aspect of the restoration, the designers attempted to balance fidelity to the original layout with the utilitarian requirements of a modern museum. While many rooms were readied for exhibits and displays, the Great Hall above all others would be treated as

BELOW: *The long journey, spent in cramped quarters without efficient food or ventilation, often took its toll on hopeful immigrants. Many never made it though the journey; others, detained due to illness, died in the island's hospital. The Ellis Island morgue, shown in its present condition, was the end of the dream for many would-be Americans.*

ABOVE: *Surrounded by new heating equipment and building material, restoration workers take a break from their duties in the sun-drenched Great Hall. Early restoration efforts concentrated on restoring the Great Hall to its nineteenth-century splendor.*

an unembelished exhibit in and of itself, restored and left as it first appeared to the immigrants. After modern facilities had been installed, the interior tile, plaster, and caen stucco facades and surfaces were cleaned and refurbished. The large first floor baggage room became the reception area, with one of the larger exhibits positioned behind it. On the second floor, the east wing is dedicated to retelling the story of the immigrant experience at Ellis Island, from their arrival through the examinations and hearings, with one of the rooms restored to its precise original appearance. The west wing exhibit chronicles the immigrant experience during the peak years of 1880-

LEFT: *The view from Ellis Island has changed drastically since the processing center closed its doors in 1954. The World Trade Center's twin towers—completed in 1976—now dominate the lower Manhattan skyline, seen here above the Wall of Honor.*

1924, detailing their journeys, processing, and settling into American life across the United States.

Miraculously, Ellis Island restoration was completed in 1990, almost two years ahead of schedule, at a total cost of $160 million. On September 9, 1990, Vice President Dan Quayle presided over the opening ceremonies, accompanied by several public figures who were instrumental in the restoration, including Lee Iacocca. On the following day, the new S.S. *Ellis Island* resumed its runs from Fort Clinton at Battery Park in Manhattan to the Ellis Island ferry slip. The masses returned.

ABOVE: *One of the many exhibits in the Ellis Island Museum that depict the experiences of particular immigrants and describe the cultural climate of America during the peak years of immigration.*

A Visit to Ellis Island Today

At the Battery Park ferry landing, under the shadow of the World Trade Center and the New York financial district, crowds gather for the 9:45 ferry, the first of the day. A seven dollar ticket will take them to the Statue of Liberty, Ellis Island, and back again. Armed with cameras, I Love NY tee-shirts, and various other mementoes purchased from vendors at the park, the broadly international crowd is entertained by

BELOW: *The new copper spires, shown here on the ground before installation, had to be lowered into place by helicopter.*

acrobats, singers, contortionists, and the ubiquitous and noisy gulls. At 9:30, two ferries pull up. The ferry with the huge line will go to the Statue of Liberty. From there, ferries to Ellis Island leave every half hour. The other, the one with the short line made up largely of park employees (and at least one freelance writer), will go directly to Ellis Island.

From late morning into afternoon, however, the halls of the main building fill rapidly with visitors fresh off the boat from the Statue of Liberty. School groups arrive for tours. A booth just inside the front door rents cordless headphones through which the recorded voice of Tom Brokaw leads a guided tour of the main building and its displays. Here, perhaps to their surprise, the visitors encounter a magnificently diverse collection

RIGHT: *The level of deterioration along with the sheer size of the buildings on Ellis Island made restorations a formidable—and expensive—undertaking.*

BELOW: *An army of photographers captured each phase of the restoration project.*

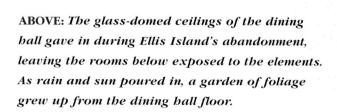

ABOVE: *The glass-domed ceilings of the dining hall gave in during Ellis Island's abandonment, leaving the rooms below exposed to the elements. As rain and sun poured in, a garden of foliage grew up from the dining hall floor.*

of exhibits, tours, films, and facilities. Large and colorful exhibits in the baggage room detail U.S. immigration history, the trends, the origins, the destinations, the overwhelming numbers. Mazes of smaller exhibits in the east and west wings capture in unforgettable visual and verbal detail the experience of particular immigrants and the environment of Ellis Island during the 1900-1914 peak years. Other startling exhibits address the role of immigrants in the making of modern America.

The entire museum is interactive. Telephones in exhibit rooms play interviews with actual immigrants. A computer installation in the baggage room allows visitors to locate names on the Wall of Honor. Upstairs in the oral history room, guests listen to hundreds of hours of interviews culled from the National Park Service's oral history project of the late 1980s. NPS librarians, oral historians, and architectural experts make themselves available for meetings by appointment. And, in the venerable grandfather of all interactive museum technologies, tour

guides, many in historical garb, lead crowds through the labyrinth of Ellis Island and immigration history.

Today's Ellis Island is a unique and dizzying place: a fully featured modern museum perfectly integrated into the very historical site it describes. While the detailed exhibits and films satisfy curiosity and the hunger for information, the echo of footsteps in the Great Hall, a sound that has probably not changed in one hundred years, appeals to something deeper, to the root of human empathy and understanding. With its heady combination of information and emotion, Ellis Island may be more challenging than most popular tourist stops. In this swirl of images and voices, the awe, the fear, and the hope felt by the immigrants are palpable. It is a place of great and often painful paradoxes: the welcoming embrace and the stern rejection, the cries of joy and the cries of sorrow, the inspiring rhetoric of "Give me your tired, your poor . . . " on one side and the difficult and forbidding language of immigration law on the other.

LEFT: *While the main building was wrapped in scaffolding during the restoration, buildings on Island 2, in the foreground, remained exposed to the elements.*

For Americans of all origins, Ellis Island is a vital reminder of the great ambitions, and imperfections, of the country's history, its visions, achievements, and contradictions. Above all, the Ellis Island National Monument honors the twelve million who passed through its gateway of hope between 1892 and 1954. It is filled with their faces, their voices, their stories, and, now, with their grateful descendants.

Index

128